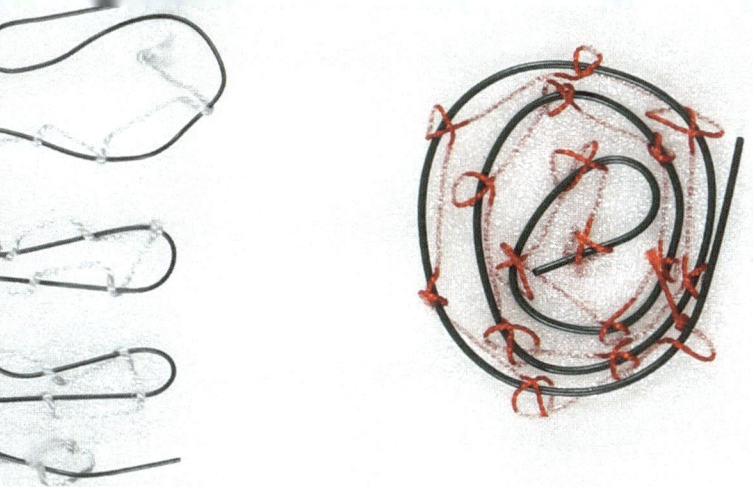

Connecting Threads

tactile social history

Lynn Setterington

*'Setterington explores the notions of craft,
form and process as social glue.'*

Professor Andrew Kötting, *UCA, Canterbury*

Cover image:
Sowing Seed (1992)
photo Michael Pollard | courtesy of the Whitworth Art Gallery

Connecting Threads © 2024 Lynn Setterington

Lynn Setterington is hereby identified as the author of this work in accordance with section 77 of the Copyright, Designs and Patent Act, 1988. She asserts and gives notice of her moral right under this Act.

Published by Quickthorn, Lower Street Atelier,
19a Lower Street, Stroud, Gloucestershire GL5 2HT UK
info@quickthornbooks.com
www.quickthornbooks.com

All rights reserved. No part of this book may be reproduced, stored in a retrieval system or transmitted in any form by any means (electronic or mechanical, through reprography, digital transmission, recording or otherwise) without prior written permission of the publisher.

Editor: Katy Bevan
Design and Typesetting: Chris J Bailey
Printed in the UK by Cambrian

Printed in the UK on uncoated FSC-certified paper

British Library Cataloguing in Publication Data applied for
ISBN: 978-1-7393160-5-1

connecting threads

Contents

Foreword p5 | Introduction p7

A sense of place: 1980s
p12

Sustainable thinking
p18

Been Shopping p22 | Stitching Up Oxford Road p24

Crossing cultures
p32

Wash Day Blues p35 | Sewing Seed p40 | Shoeshine p42

Identity and belonging
p44

Sreepur Quilt p49 | Remembering Emily p52 | Signature Bags p60

Threads of Identity p63 | Sew Near – Sew Far p68

Health and wellbeing
p76

Respect and Protect p79 | Safety Net p83 | Living with Loss p90

Running a community project
p92

Glossary of terms p94

Works in collections p95

Been Shopping, repurposed plastic bags (2005) | photo Lynn Setterington

Foreword

I have been following Lynn Setterington's career since the early 1990s. By then she was already admired for her engagement with kanthas, in the form of Bangladeshi recycled and embroidered cloths. That these ordinary objects from women's lives resonated with her, was evident in her work, leading me to write: 'Her rhythmic stitches are stamped with an urgency, a pervasive insistence which is far removed from the European tradition of embroidery; instead they place Lynn Setterington's work within the realm of that relatively new form of urban naïve art, best known through minimalist music and dance…'

As it has turned out, this embrace of repetition as a creative expression has underpinned her dual goals. These intertwine the desire to create a fairer, more equitable society with the urge to listen and enable different voices – and importantly, ordinary voices – to be heard. Ultimately, through her flexible approach, aptitude for dealing with uncertainty, ability to tread carefully and adapt, she has had a quiet but forceful impact, creating performance pieces that, as she notes in this book, rendered her an 'ethnographic embroiderer, with fieldwork, empathy and an understanding of place' as central to the resulting artistry, which she likens rightly to social history documents.

Unusually, in a career that has garnered international recognition, Setterington remains modest, committed to the next collaboration, the sharing of textile languages, the rituals of ordinary life. Hand stitch remains at the heart of all this. As she notes: 'Embroidery today is celebrated, practised and appreciated by people from all different backgrounds and walks of life, and its value as a connecting thread and vital accessible global communication tool is finally being recognised.' What must be added is that this recognition has been urged forward by Setterington herself. Reflecting back to my own comment about dance, there is no doubt that with her sensitivity to signatures as individual gestures, curiosity that catalyses engagement with a diverse array of people and projects, and the enabling of sensory engagement essential to wellbeing, she is a choreographer par excellence.

Mary Schoeser
Textile historian and co-founder of the School of Textiles

above: **Sowing Seed** | photo Michael Pollard | courtesy of the Whitworth Art Gallery
right: **portrait of the author** | photo Eddie Setterington

Introduction

'Stitches are a means to an end in needlework, not an end in themselves. They are the words of our needle language, without them we cannot speak.'

Gladys Windsor Fry, *Embroidery and Needlework, 1935:3*

Connecting Threads brings together twelve textile projects completed between 1981 and 2024. Each one acts as a social history document, providing tactile evidence of – often untold – stories of people on the margins, unexamined histories and overlooked places through stitch.

The resulting work is both personal and political. It ranges from tiny colourful hand embroidered fragments recording everyday life in south London and Yorkshire, to monumental, site-specific banners made with construction workers in the north of England.

As a collection, it describes my life in stitch detailing how an artist-embroiderer works and thinks creatively, how projects are managed and take shape and some of the hurdles encountered in socially engaged practice. The projects described in this book encompass themes of identity and belonging, health and wellbeing, sustainability, community cohesion and social inequality, offering sensory testaments of life today.

Putting this book together has provided me with an opportunity to re-examine an extensive and sustained body of work. It has enabled me to see commonalities

and connections across and between diverse projects and to appreciate the small but significant details of life sewn into different surfaces. These markers of identity acknowledge people and events in soft, transportable objects that detail belonging.

It has also allowed me to revisit work I have not seen for many years. Seeing some of these textiles again has been like encountering old friends – the stitched surfaces recalling people, places and connections. The cloths are holders of memories, with each stitch a unique record, a sensory reminder.

There is overlap and a blurring of boundaries across and between the projects, hand stitch being the unifying element with myself, the artist, as the connecting thread. Viewed together, these projects raise awareness of living sustainably, whether through the reuse of materials or in the depictions of allotment life. They also highlight some of the delights – and pitfalls – of shared making, something which I hope will be useful for others interested in engaging in craft collaborations. However, important though these aspects are, at their core, the tactile commemorations that make up *Connecting Threads* are a celebration of humanity. The act of stitching with thread in a group setting and the resulting thread mark that detail, the ordinary, and often extraordinary, stories of the people involved in their making are vital evidence that we are here, that we belong.

Shared making: stitch is a collaborative process

I have navigated the complexities of community-focused projects throughout my career, first as a solo maker and then as a socially engaged artist. In the 1990s, I worked with Asian women's groups. We found we shared an interest in kantha work (kantha is a form of embroidery or quilting made with running stitch). Opportunities to work in the wider community with hard-to-reach groups, adults with learning disabilities and school children followed and I also worked with refugee charities, where stitch proved useful as a vital, common shared language to be used creatively. In these encounters, stitching functioned as sensory mark making. In others, when working with construction workers and the mental health charity MIND for example, sewing was channelled into a wellbeing strategy. Stitch has always been an important means of communication for me, and each of these projects fostered a creative conduit between people, locally and globally.

Shared making is a complex process and the resolved artwork is just one piece of a complex jigsaw, a subject little discussed in academic research or funding applications. Although creating with others is a strategy that can yield rich rewards, it may also elicit challenges and dilemmas for the artist-instigator. As well as initiating projects,

World Mental Health Day workshop at Manchester Metropolitan University (2021) | photo Clare Calveley

they must also act as a facilitator, activist, designer, maker, co-ordinator, over-seer and occasionally confidante too. Even the workshop setting may represent more than just a creative space for some participants, coming instead to symbolise an escape from home, a safe environment, a place to gain new skills, meet people or avoid the stresses of everyday life.

The role of the socially engaged artist has been described as that of choreographer or conductor; someone with knowledge and expertise who can guide and oversee the work and manage the teams involved in the shared outcome. It requires skill, patience and expertise, but also the ability to know when to step back so that people do not feel intimidated. Devising a collaborative creative project that is broad and engaging, of value to potential participants but at the same time relevant to the wider art world is a real skill and challenge. Bringing the two worlds together requires careful planning and research. As anthropologist Sarah Pink puts it in her book, *Doing Sensory Ethnography* (Sage, 2009): 'Creative research and material thinking is itself often an intuitive, messy and sometimes serendipitous task'.

Julia Puebla Fortier, an academic with many years of experience in this arena, is developing some timely research at the London School of Hygiene and Tropical Medicine into how to support socially engaged artists so they do not burn out with the stresses of shared working. She is one of a handful of academics to be directing their gaze this way; speaking to artists, rather than the community, about the impact this way of working has on their own wellbeing.

So, what does real co-design look like? Is there such a thing and how do you navigate the twists and turns in collective working when people are invested in different outcomes? Co-design and co-production are buzzwords that suggest equality and inclusion, but these noble objectives may be hard to realise fully in practice. For instance, should all voices be equal?

Maintaining the quality of the finished piece while encouraging the broadest level of participation is a balancing act. Stitch as a method is inclusive and, overall, non-threatening as an art form and its take-up and visibility has grown exponentially over the last decade. It has been embraced by many wishing to explore community and working together, from those well versed in textile methods to experts in other fields such as cultural geographers, poets and speech therapists. Each one brings different skills and agendas. In some cases, the act of working together is the main driver. In the case of wellbeing initiatives, the aesthetic outcome is often of secondary significance.

In many of the projects explored in this book, the visual outcome is crucial – as is meaning and visual integrity; however the resulting artwork should be judged differently to a solo initiative where only one voice is heard. The many unseen values in shared making should, ideally, be recorded in some way so that these hidden benefits can be acknowledged alongside the resulting textile.

Stitch as a collaborative process can be used and developed in different ways, depending on the groups involved and the subject under scrutiny. For example, in 2009, I worked with a group from Manchester MIND. Our shared discussions made us realise that this project was less about sewing and more about talking and empowering the female participants, so we decided to create a communal quilt. The sessions not only enabled the group to share ideas, but also gave the women a reason to meet regularly, share ideas informally and work without any pressure – very much like the five steps to wellbeing (to connect, to be active, to take note, to keep learning, to give), developed by The New Economics Foundation in 2008 in relation to mental health. Stitch as a wellbeing strategy is often associated with slow working, mindfulness and repetition. However, this is not something I focus on in my projects, and I do not specify stitch skills as a prerequisite.

I regard my role as that of an ethnographic embroiderer, with fieldwork, empathy and

Lynn Setterington installing Sew Near, Haworth Moors, Yorkshire (2017) | photo Jonathan Turner

understanding place key to the process of creating. Empathy is a method employed and embraced by anthropologists: listening, observing and paying attention to others are all skills developed over many years. Working with others inevitably links to issues of consent, privilege and power relations, concerns which, as artist Suzanne Lacey acknowledges in her 1994 book *Mapping the Terrain*, are 'exposed in the process of creating'. Similarly, anthropologist Soyini Madison argues that the representation of others, 'is always going to be a complicated and contentious undertaking' (2012:4) and I have come to appreciate that sensitivity is paramount in the collective making process.

The twelve projects described in the following pages highlight a range of themes and provide a way into a much larger body of stitched, pieced and quilted cloths. So much has changed since the first pieces were made in the early 1980s. Embroidery today is no longer on the margins. It is celebrated, explored and appreciated by people from all different backgrounds and walks of life, and its value as a connecting thread and vital accessible global communication tool is finally becoming more widely recognised.

Lynn Setterington

A sense of place: 1980s

connecting threads

Leeds Market, hand and machine stitch (1984) | photo Lynn Setterington (2023)

A sense of place: 1980s

'These hand-sewn documents are tangible reminders of past lives and add to an alternative, sensory representation of British history...'

These small intimate embroideries provide a narrative record in thread of my life in the early 1980s. They capture everyday stories and detail the transition from my life in a small Yorkshire village to living and studying in the capital. The brightly coloured stitch fragments celebrate the rituals of ordinary life, a theme I have reinterpreted over the years, and the images include bustling street scenes, a game of bingo on the seafront at Scarborough and shoppers going about their business in the Victorian market hall in Leeds. All these places have changed in recent decades, so these hand-sewn documents are tangible reminders of past lives and add to an alternative, sensory representation of British history going back to the Bayeux Tapestry.

Each of these early embroideries is irregular in shape, purposefully crooked and uneven like a tiny fragment of life. Fabrics and yarns are intuitive responses for me – whether a scrap of cloth left over from dressmaking or a thread that lends the right colour, texture or surface quality.

Similarly, there is no adherence to specialist yarns or particular types of stitch. Different yarn types and qualities are embraced and as long as they can be threaded through a needle, I will try to sew with them. I value tactility and versatility and the vast choice of colour, feel and texture available in sewing, knitting and crochet yarns can be equated to drawing with different tools. Just as you might determine a broad spectrum of texture, line quality, colour, opacity and atmosphere through the use of charcoal sticks, oil pastels or ink pens, the same principles apply when working with thread. A boucle wool yarn will give a textured effect; a straight, smooth raffia thread looks and behaves very differently. There are so many possible weights, textures and variations of yarn and thread – matt or shiny, manmade or natural, variegated, stranded or single ply. My overall approach was, and remains, governed by instinct and feel. This impulse sits within the shared work too.

It is noticeable to me now, that the colour in these early pieces is heightened, something which perhaps found its inspiration in archive sources. (These are an important

Small hand-stitched embroideries (1980–84)
photo Lynn Setterington

factor in both my solo and shared projects to this day.) Visits to museums including the Victoria and Albert, the Horniman and British Museum were a regular occurrence and the illuminated manuscripts, Coptic textiles and ancient frescos I looked at offered a glimpse into other worlds and lives. Historic textiles and folk art in local and national museums across the world have also remained a constant source of inspiration.

Electric Avenue, hand embroidery (1981) | photo David Bennett

Electric Avenue (1981)

This small hand embroidery captures the street life of Brixton, celebrating the atmosphere of this working-class area of south-west London. Electric Avenue in Brixton was – and still is – a street market and in the early 1980s it was part of a bustling, vibrant multicultural community. It was a stark contrast to the monoculture of the small Yorkshire village I came from.

The atmosphere of place is documented in a mix of media, a different way to capture the vibrancy of London. Electric Avenue is intuitive, using the texture and colour of the threads to portray an everyday scene. The frayed edges and irregular shape add texture and also speak to the fractured nature of this small piece of social history. They also nod to frescos and fragments of history found in museums worldwide.

Brixton Market, hand embroidery (1981)
photo David Bennett

connecting threads

**Bingo (Scarborough),
hand embroidery (1981)**
photo David Bennett

London street, oil pastel drawing
photo David Bennett

Bingo (1981)

Bingo is a narrative textile. It tells the story of the British seaside and celebrates the small rituals of ordinary life. Like Electric Avenue, it captures the bustle and vibrancy of working-class culture. The sea front scene is a snapshot of the everyday; people are coming and going and having fun. The stitching is free and direct with threads chosen instinctively, based on colour and feel. The embroidery is worked into a small scrap of rust-coloured corduroy taken from a dress fabric. The raw edge of the cloth adds to the overall aesthetic and composition.

connecting threads

Sustainable thinking

Colour sample (2006) | photo Jason Lees

connecting threads

Sustainable thinking

'Been Shopping twenty years on is a stark reminder of how much the high street has changed...'

The history of textiles is complex and their inventive repurposing, often driven by necessity, has been part of our collective narrative for centuries. The first recorded patchwork quilt in England was created in the 18th century from scraps of Indian imported cottons and is on display in Levens Hall in Cumbria. Shoddy blankets, another method of recycling, were first created in the early 19th century in Batley, West Yorkshire using a newly-invented process that shredded existing fabrics. The Second World War mantra of 'Make do and Mend' has also been well documented. In the face of shortages, women were championed for the ingenuity and skill with which they reworked old clothes and textiles.

The Suffolk puff adds to this story. Dating back to the 17th century, traditional Suffolk puffs (the unusual name is said to derive from the technique's origins in the county) are hand sewn from waste fabric. The material is cut into roundels and a running stitch is used to gather the cloth into a circle, unit or module of fabric. The gathering-up process reconfigures the patterned fabric, transforming it into something new and different and repeating this process allows you to create numerous circles, each one unique. The colourful, circular units are then joined together to make a new textile such as a quilt or occasionally an edge feature on a garment or blanket. It is a slow and time-consuming process, but the repeat action creates a gentle rhythm and something of a mindful strategy.

Like many textile processes, Suffolk puffs have been adapted and have transformed over time – in the USA, they are known as 'yo-yos' – and examples of this vernacular art form can be sought out in museum collections both in the UK and abroad. The Rachel Kay-Shuttleworth Collection housed at Gawthorpe Hall in Lancashire has historic examples, and in the US they are well represented in public collections, for example the San Jose Museum of Quilts and Textiles and Birmingham Museum of Art, Alabama.

Plastic bag donations, Stitching Up Oxford Road (2006) | photo Jason Lees

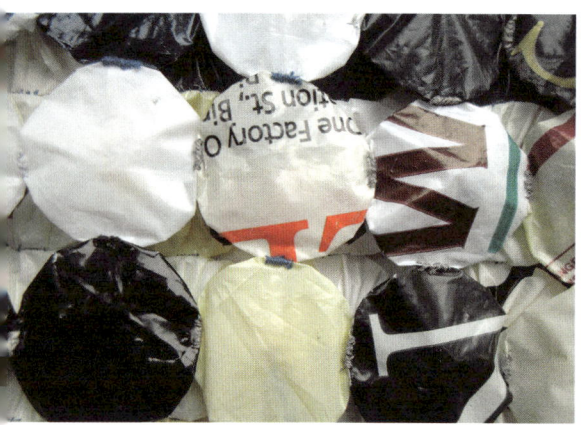

top: **Been Shopping on a green ground (2004)**
photo Stephen Yates
middle: **Shop detail, repurposed plastic bags (2005)**
photo Lynn Setterington
bottom: **Back view of Been Shopping**
photo Lynn Setterington

Been Shopping (2004)

Been Shopping is a wry commentary on consumerism and our ever-growing interest in retail therapy. The cloth is made up of Suffolk puffs created from recycled plastic carrier bags.

The idea of using plastic bags to make Suffolk puffs began in the early 2000s when these materials were plentiful and available in a wide range of colours and designs, This approach evolved through work with Venture Arts, an organisation based in Hulme, Manchester that partners with artists with learning disabilities (www.venturearts.org). Running a creative allotment arts class at Venture Arts where the outcomes would be shown in the local community garden centre was a new challenge. We had little money for materials and, given that we were showing the work outside, the usual fabric sources were not appropriate. A solution was found in a stash of brightly coloured plastic bags and we set about reconfiguring the manmade material using different textile processes, including weaving, stitching collage and wrapping.

Out of all the textile techniques we explored, it was the Suffolk puffs that seemed the most interesting and effective. The gathered circles transformed the ordinary plastic into a material that resembled indigo-dyed fabrics and Japanese cloths, with many unusual and varied patterns emerging. And in using plastic, which does not fray, we could avoid one of the disadvantages of traditional Suffolk puff making – the laborious step of turning an edge on the cloth circle.

Been Shopping (2004) | photo Stephen Yates

Another feature of Suffolk puff quilts is that the reverse side of the cloth creates a textured surface and the work can be displayed so that both sides are visible.

The colour palette for Been Shopping was predetermined by our personal shopping habits. The predominance of white, yellow, navy and brown plastic bags reflected the shops I visited and bought clothes from at that time and, like most of the quilts and embroideries featured here, mark a moment in time. The same applies to traditional patchwork quilts; if you were to unpick a cloth, you could work out the date of its creation through the materials used in its construction. Looking at Been Shopping twenty years on is a stark reminder of how much the high street has changed, reflecting the vagaries of consumerism and shopping.

Stitching Up Oxford Road, work in progress (2006) | photo Jason Lees

Stitching Up Oxford Road (2006)

Stitching Up Oxford Road was a commission in 2006 funded by the Higher Education Funding Council working with Manchester Metropolitan University (MMU) to bring together diverse communities on Oxford Road, a busy thoroughfare in the city. It was a forerunner to a larger and more complex undertaking a few years later to scale back traffic on this polluted corridor and turn it into an urban greenway. (Today it is indeed a pleasant and tranquil space.)

There were multiple outcomes from Stitching Up Oxford Road and this new, co-operative way of working initiated to a step change in my practice, signposting new collaborative and shared approaches, many of which remain in place today. It led to the development of ethnographic strategies in which artists become embedded in a place to understand the people they are working with and the issues they face.

This project was also a catalyst in developing sustainable making and sharing good accessible practice, shining a light on the intricacies of working together. (The appreciation of a reliable and skilled team was crucial in this complex undertaking to help navigate the hurdles in social making.) It also highlighted absence, drawing attention to people who may be missing in such narratives. Doing drop-in workshops in a hospital setting was not always easy, for example, most people were waiting for an appointment and as a result were somewhat anxious. In hindsight, after speaking to hospital managers in more depth, it might have been more beneficial to plan the sessions in advance.

In the early 2000s, when this project took place, Manchester's Oxford Road was a noisy and polluted thoroughfare leading into the city centre. It was home to many prestigious institutions, including two universities, Manchester Royal Infirmary, the Whitworth Art Gallery, the Aquatics Centre and the BBC, but all were very separate entities. Our proposal focused on uniting the communities using sustainable methods in the creation of a large-scale community quilt made from recycled plastic bags donated by people living and working in the vicinity. Having devised and made two earlier quilts using Suffolk puffs fashioned from plastic bags, (Recycle Carrier Bags and Been Shopping) the process was tried and tested. The brief fitted the ambitions of the funders, which were to unite creatively some of the diverse organisations and institutions on Oxford Road, and so the commission was awarded. The project employed deliberately low tech, inclusive and flexible methods so that it could be transported and worked on by different audiences on Oxford Road.

Pankhurst Centre workshop with Amy Gunawan (2006)
photo Lynn Setterington

With its emphasis on recycling plastic, it was also a timely opportunity to raise awareness of an important societal issue: statistics showed that in 2005 the average person used up to 134 plastic carrier bags a year.

The timeframe was fixed and limited, so everything had to happen quickly. The commission was awarded in December 2005 and the work had to be completed by April 2006. The first key task was to get partner organisations on board and make sure as many different venues were involved as possible. Having used the Suffolk puff method already, there was a sound understanding of what was involved in the creative sessions so all the hosts would be asked to do was provide a suitable space with a table to run a workshop; we would provide everything else. Walking up and down Oxford Road with colourful samples and images of the earlier outcomes was a good way to entice others to join in and this sensory approach also allowed us to observe the flow of day-to-day activities along the road, from school children at bus stops at 3pm, students queuing at music venues, staff and patients coming and going from Manchester Royal Infirmary and visitors leaving museums and galleries.

The first planned visit was to the Whitworth Art Gallery to see if they would like to be involved. This was a pragmatic choice given that it has a world-renowned textile collection. Thankfully the gallery was keen, and having a high-profile venue as a partner helped when approaching subsequent organisations and venues. In the end we amassed a total of sixteen participating venues ranging from the Deaf Institute, the Gay and Lesbian Centre, Eighth Day vegetarian café, Manchester Museum, the Aquatics Centre and the BBC. Once the venues were in place, we scheduled a series of workshops aiming to vary the times and days of week so as many people as possible could take part.

It soon became clear that with the short time frame and workshops happening concurrently in different venues, more than one person would be needed to help run the workshops and share in the making and creative thinking. We recruited three recent embroidery graduates, Mark Beecroft, Richard McVetis and Karen Moran as co-workers who were joined by a documentary photographer, Jason Lees and Sam Gray, a colleague at MMU. Sam, with his role at the University, was a good sounding board. Calm and supportive he was able to liaise with the funders and help plan the celebration event.

Having secured the venues, one of the first practical steps was to collect the donated

connecting threads

plastic bags. This was in the days before social media so we created a simple flyer sharing the locations of the collection bins and details of all the public workshops and distributed it on and around Oxford Road. This helped raise awareness of the project and brought chance into the equation – the material base and colour palette of the quilt were dependent on donated plastic bags. It was a risky strategy that meant we would have to think on our feet and adapt to the choices presented to us. Once the collection bins were emptied, we laid out all the bags so we could see and feel the different types of plastics and examine the range of typography, colours and shapes we had to work with.

The workshops were divided between the four workers, plus some embroidery student helpers. Two students made a sample from biodegradable plastic bags. Colleagues in the science dept at MMU confirmed that we needed to avoid this plastic in the final artwork as its inclusion would affect the strength and longevity of the artwork.

Two other unplanned adaptations happened when the project was publicised in the local press. Firstly, we were approached by who someone who wanted to be involved in the making process, but at a distance, so plastic bags were taken to her home for her to work with. And secondly, we were given a bin liner full of colour-coded carrier bags, collected by a former primary school teacher who wanted to share her hoard. Comprising bags from Marks & Spencer/St Michael shopping bags in many different shades of green to ones for companies no longer trading, this collection was a wonderful piece of social history; a poignant reminder of commercial businesses of the past and the transitory nature of consumerism.

Stitching Up Oxford Road was also important in highlighting the way that the artist in such projects functions as the connecting thread between people and organisations; a privileged and unique viewpoint that can be used positively. Creative projects such as this provide an easy and direct way to share information and when exploring sensitive subjects (such as health related topics), challenging information can be disseminated in a different way as the craft making takes place.

At the making workshop, leaflets and newspaper articles about the impact of plastic waste on the environment provided information and a talking point, so even if people did not want to participate in making, or were accompanied by someone who didn't, they could still learn something about the circular economy and the sustainable living agenda.

connecting threads

Whitworth Art Gallery workshop with (l-r) Nigel Hurlstone, Ann Gibson, Janet Bezzant and Amy Gunawan (2006) | photo Lynn Setterington

Transporting Stitching Up Oxford Road to different venues (2006) | photo Lynn Setterington

As the workshops settled into a rhythm, and we began to amass collections of Suffolk puffs, it was useful to come together to view the contributions and begin to explore ways to take the quilt/ banner forward. (The approach of creating units allowed some flexibility and opened up different ways to think about and construct a shared outcome.) Together we laid out the circles of colour using the Humanities building at MMU. This was a perfect space with a large atrium so we could climb the stairs and see the work from a distance.

We laid the circles in different configurations and finally agreed on an idea – the units of colour would spell out 'Manchester Oxford Road'. The circles were bold, vibrant and each was unique, so it was clear that the composition did not need to be complicated, the work spoke for itself. This text-based outcome resonated with both my earlier quilts created from plastic and with historical trade union banners. As it grew, it took on its own character, resembling both an ancient mosaic floor and a modern digital design with the circular modules reminiscent of pixels.

This shared session was also useful in helping to calculate roughly how many new Suffolk puffs still needed to be made in the remaining workshops. However, this stage also brought a moral dilemma, should we include the whole range of Suffolk puffs created in the workshops or select only the

Composing the quilt at MMU; (l-r) Richard McVetis, Mark Beecroft, Nigel Hurlstone, Lynn Setterington and Karen Moran (2006) | photo Jason Lees

best examples? This is something Grant Kester highlights in *The One and the Many* (2011:10) questioning 'how do we determine which transgressions matter in socially engaged arts?'

In Stitching Up Oxford Road, we discussed the options and, in the end, decided to leave out any puffs that were not well executed. This was a pragmatic decision because including puffs that were not well sewn would impact the construction, strength and ultimately the life span of the cloth.

Exploring different compositions, All Saints, MMU (2006) | photo Lynn Setterington

The final stitch up in All Saints, MMU: (l-r) Karen Moran, Richard McVetis and Mark Beecroft (2006) | photo Lynn Setterington

The resolved textile banner was put up over a two-week period. The thirty-four letters were divided between the team of four, who sewed the cloth together by hand. Each letter or block was uniform, made up of eighty Suffolk puffs, ten by eight rows. Sewing the individual blocks together first meant we could explore different layouts before the whole cloth was joined together and it also gave us time to document these compositions in locations on Oxford Road.

Another aspect that is unique to the construction of a Suffolk Puff cloth is that the resulting fabric is not a solid mass, with gaps between the joined circles. This means that the surface onto which the quilt is displayed affects the dynamic of the artwork.

Made up of over 3,000 hand sewn motifs, Stitching Up Oxford Road was displayed at Manchester Metropolitan University in April 2006. Alongside it were photographs of the workshops in different settings. All those involved were invited to the opening event and each venue was presented with a poster of the finished quilt. The quilt remained on Oxford Road in the MMU Vice Chancellor's office for ten years and when he retired, it was donated it to the Whitworth Art Gallery so that it would remain on Oxford Road. Seeing it again twenty years on, it remains vibrant and bold and proudly demonstrates how working together can lead to multiple new, unexpected, creative and rewarding results.

connecting threads

Revisiting Stitching Up (18 years on) in the Whitworth Collection (2024) | photo Lynn Setterington

Richard McVetis said of the project: 'Being part of Stitching Up Oxford Road allowed me to challenge myself, learn new skills and gain experience, helping me grow personally and professionally. It was an opportunity to explore a different way of working, engage with a diverse audience and test my confidence. Working with an established practitioner was inspiring and motivating.'

Karen Moran said: 'Participating in Stitching Up Oxford Road was an edifying experience. The process of stitching together Suffolk Puffs from plastic cuttings not only enhanced my artistic skills but also made me think differently about waste and its impact. It was inspiring to see how a harmful product could be repurposed into something meaningful and thought provoking, fostering a sense of collective creativity and environmental consciousness within the Oxford Road community.'

connecting threads

Crossing cultures

The Reverie of Objects (1994) pencil drawing | photo David Bennett

connecting threads

Crossing cultures

'My hand-sewn cloths celebrate women's lives, depicting in thread those commonplace items that we use all the time and take for granted.'

y interest in kanthas began after a visit to the Woven Air exhibition at The Whitechapel Gallery in 1988. Kantha embroidery/quilting originated in the Bengal area in what is now Bangladesh and India and the earliest kanthas were made in the late 19th century from old saris and dhotis, carefully pieced together to make a new cloth, the size and shape of which depended on its purpose. These textiles were not initially made commercially and their use varied from ritual objects to protective covers for precious items – when the state of Bangladesh was formed in 1971, the kantha was so highly respected that one was used to wrap the constitution.

Made exclusively by women, these kanthas constitute an important part of traditional folk art encompassing, in the early examples, both Hindu and Muslim religions as well as regional links between India and what was to become Bangladesh.

Kantha work also celebrates simple rural life in this part of the world through the depiction of day-to-day activities, from rice winnowing to fishing and hunting. Unlike sashiko embroidery and boro textiles from Japan, kanthas are more varied, featuring narratives alongside geometric stitch designs as well as non-representational designs.

The workmanship of some of the early quilts is quite breathtaking. The range of stitched stories, motifs and styles is captivating, ranging from beautiful, naïve folk imagery to sophisticated and complicated narrative dramas detailing the life of Krishna and other Indian deities. Some border patterns are skilfully worked, the stitches created to look like they were designed on a loom imitating woven cloth. In contrast, some of the non-figurative cloths made by Muslim women use these border patterns as a main surface decoration.

The Whitechapel Gallery was the first UK venue to showcase the textile expertise of Bengal, and the Woven Air exhibition highlighted two very different textile processes the region was known for: hand-stitched quilts, referred to as 'nakshi' kanthas, and woven cloth – specifically the fine muslin that inspired the exhibition's title, Woven Air.

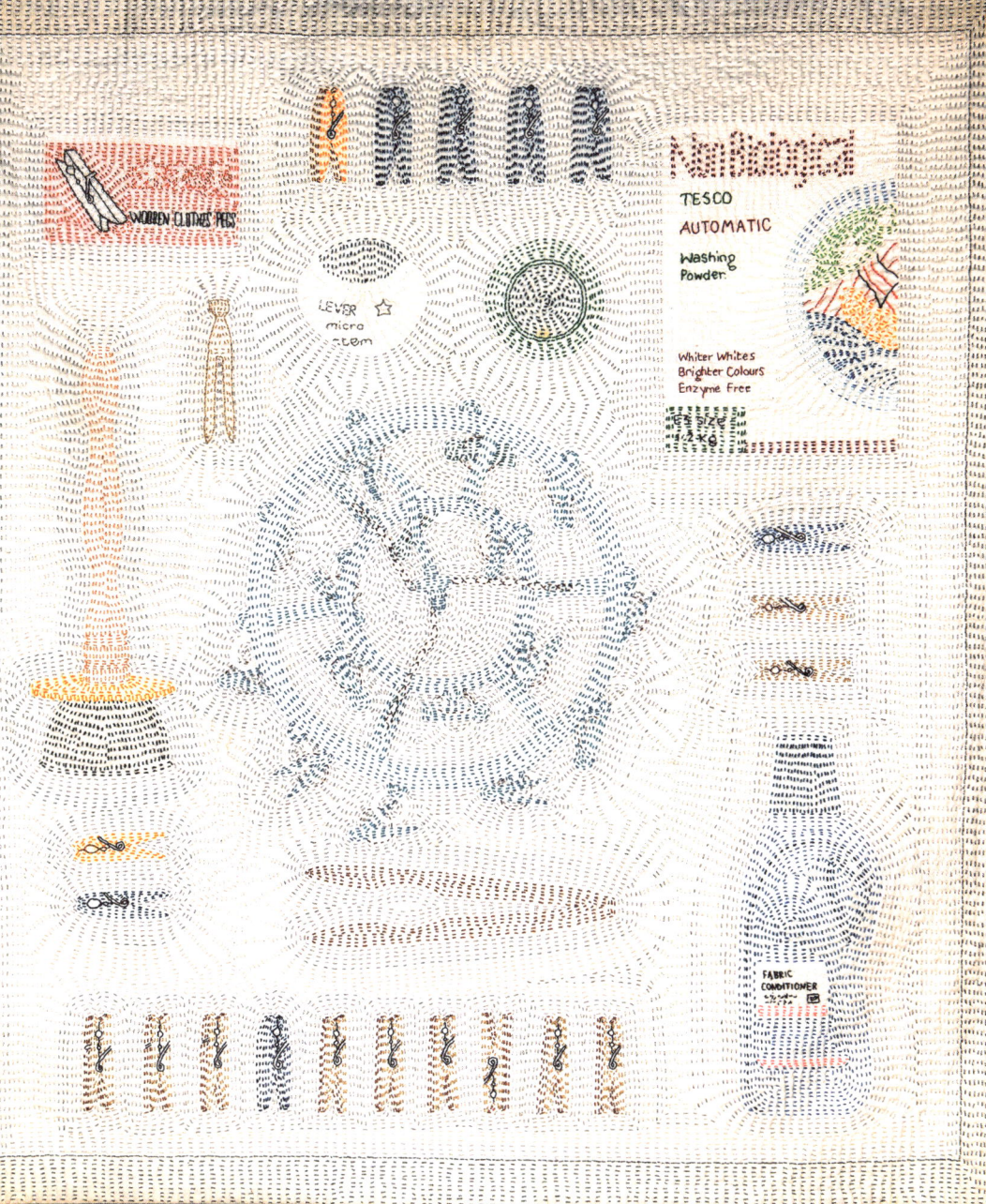

Washday Blues (1994) | photo Ian Lillicrapp, courtesy of The Embroiderers' Guild

Wash Day Blues (early 1990s)

This quilt captures a little-documented ritual of domestic life depicting past and present tools and objects associated with this never-ending and ongoing chore. I have always been fascinated by these everyday items and try to imagine what someone from the future would make of redundant tools. For example, the wooden tongs featured that were used to grab

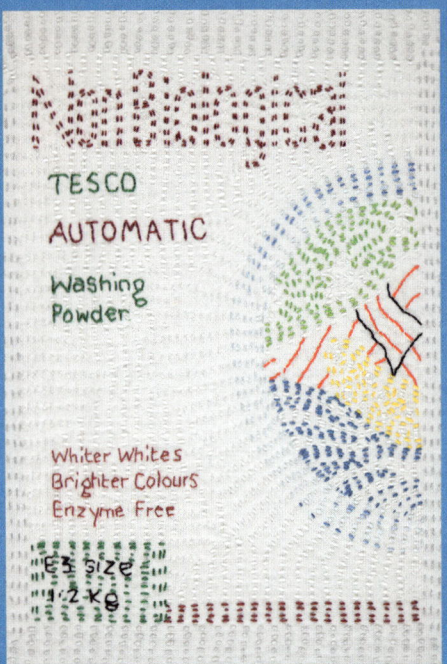

clothes from hot water before the invention of automatic washing machines. The quilt's composition is arranged to resemble a modern-day front-loading washing machine, the central circular door re-imagined as a plastic clothes hanger to dry small items such as socks, knickers and bras, echoing once more the mandala found in early kanthas from Bengal. Wooden pegs are a reminder of my childhood, with plastic ones in all shapes and colours the norm today. Other items portrayed in thread are a sink plunger, washing detergent containers, fabric conditioner and the washing powder itself.

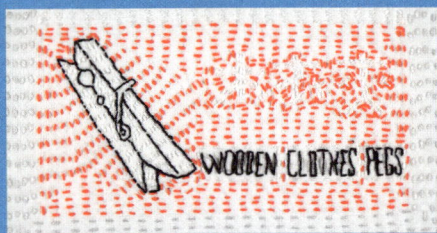

Details from Washday Blues (1994) | photos Ian Lillicrapp, courtesy of The Embroiderers' Guild

Kantha drawing pencil on black paper (1994)
photo David Bennett

The gallery worked strategically to draw in the local community. Back then, the Brick Lane area was home to factories, warehouses and suppliers linked to the fashion, or rag, trade, providing a livelihood for around 60,000 Bangladeshis.

The beauty, variety and intensity of the hand stitching in these wonderful objects was a revelation to me. This type of textile was barely known in Europe at that time, with very few examples in British collections, so it was pure joy to closely examine the inventive way the women stitched patterns and elaborate imagery in thread. I loved the fact that there was often no correct orientation to the work, which could be

Kantha drawing, pencil on black paper (1994) | photo David Bennett

viewed just as well upside down, or from the side. They were made not as pieces of wall art but as ritual objects to be used in different ways and settings. With my love of folk art, hand stitch and the everyday, these cloths resonated with my own practice. I was drawn to the use of recycled materials, with saris and threads reused extensively to make new and varied creations.

I realised that the women used many forms of running stitch to create the cloths and that numerous visual effects could be achieved by spacing the rows of stitches differently. Some women used diagonal stitches to create a step-like line, while others worked stitches in blocks, resulting in a checkerboard pattern. Shapes were often outlined in back stitch or with a more subtle, broken line made from running stitch. No two pieces were alike; each cloth was a unique way of drawing with stitch, highlighting different compositions, approaches and styles.

The images of mundane objects stitched into cloth echoed my own work. At the time, I was drawing and embroidering ubiquitous domestic objects that are used by women every day yet are often overlooked, such as teapots and kitchen utensils. The fact that the women have sewn images of earrings, combs and mirrors into the kantha quilts connected with my own work. My hand-sewn cloths celebrate women's

Sultana Kantha | photo Lynn Setterington

lives, depicting in thread those commonplace items that we use all the time and take for granted.

Inspired by all I had seen, I went home and began using a running stitch to create pictures of objects from my own domestic surroundings; an iron, a seed packet, pairs of earrings. I loved the way this approach looked; the stitch marks created unusual optical effects, reminiscent of pointillism, and the outcomes were so different to how I had worked before, yet it matched my uncomplicated, accessible mantra.

Kotha and Kantha workshop, Manchester library (2026) | photo Lynn Setterington

Kotha and Kantha outcomes (2016) | photo Lynn Setterington

I sought out the work of Stella Kramrisch at the British Museum. Kramrisch was a leading scholar in Indian art history who amassed a collection of kanthas in the early 20th century through her work in Calcutta. *Kantha; the embroidered quilts of Bengal* (2013) edited by Darielle Mason, is an excellent visual publication detailing an exhibition at Philadelphia Museum, which showcased this collection alongside another belonging to Jill and Sheldon Bonovitz. I was fascinated by these early cloths and my research led me to visit to Bangladesh in 1995, forging a connection that has been sustained and developed through my work with Sreepur Village, a small charity in Bangladesh (see p49) and many other stitch-based workshops across the globe.

Kotha and Kantha

The Bangladeshi Women's Memoir Project, was run during 2016 with the Ahmed Iqbal Ullah Education Trust and the playwright and teacher Dipali Das. Two sets of six workshops took place over a period of four months. The project combined stitching with biographical writing. 'Kotha' means lines, or writing in Bengali, and 'Kantha' is stitches, so embroidery and writing were combined in the project.

connecting threads

top: **Sewing Seed with oil pastel drawing with hosepipe on paper (1995)** | photo David Bennett
bottom: **Sewing Seed sketch with pencil drawing with hosepipe on black paper (1995)** | photo David Bennett

These two sketches are all that remain from a quilt, one of four, that disappeared from a show at New Brewery Arts, Cirencester, in 1996.

Sewing Seed (1991)

Sewing Seed is a large kantha quilt, created as a tribute to my first year as an allotment holder. Through its depiction in thread of tools and the paraphernalia associated with allotments and growing your own, it celebrates a love of gardening, family and sustainable living.

The quilt is imbued with family memories, particularly of my father who died a few years before this cloth was created. He was a rural science teacher and his presence is palpable in the objects stitched into the cloth. Allotments are now embraced by people of all ages, but back in the early 1990s, they were seen as something other; just for old people. Not put off and proud of my new acquisition, I was glad to have somewhere green to go in London where I could dig the earth and I wanted to share this passion with others. These community green spaces have immense value and provide enjoyment for our physical and mental health.

In traditional kanthas, the centre of the cloth is marked with a circular image in the form of a lotus flower or mandala, celebrating the cycle of life, rebirth and regeneration. Sometimes trees of life are also angled in from the corners of the cloth, pointing towards the central motif and adding more elements to the composition.

In Sewing Seed, traditional images and icons are replaced by Western symbols of regrowth and regeneration, including seed packets, a hosepipe and a watering can, all proudly positioned in the centre of the cloth. Some objects are turned upside down as a homage to the non-directional orientation of a kantha.

This quilt marks a moment in time detailing, in coloured threads, the many items connected to allotment life: a trowel, a flask, wellington boots, a radio, some secateurs. Not only is the placement of objects important, but the dialogue and space between the objects is also crucial. Everything in the composition is of equal value, which gives it egality and serenity, allowing the eye to travel freely across the rippled surface to view the patterns created around and between. The richly textured surface qualities and optical effects created by the intense repetitive stitching bring something quite different to traditional western quilt making and textile iconography.

Colour is another vital element in a kantha. The colour palette, although seemingly subtle, includes strong tones but the process of stitching through the quilted surface disperses the coloured yarns, making them appear less intense and bold. The relationship between colours and sewn motifs can change and shift as the surface is filled with stitches, connecting the fore and background.

Sewing Seed is framed by borders made from stitch patterns sewn at regular intervals, once again drawing on traditional kantha motifs. Often the borders were designed to imitate weave patterns and, in some cases, it is almost impossible to distinguish the complex stitch designs from a loom woven cloth.

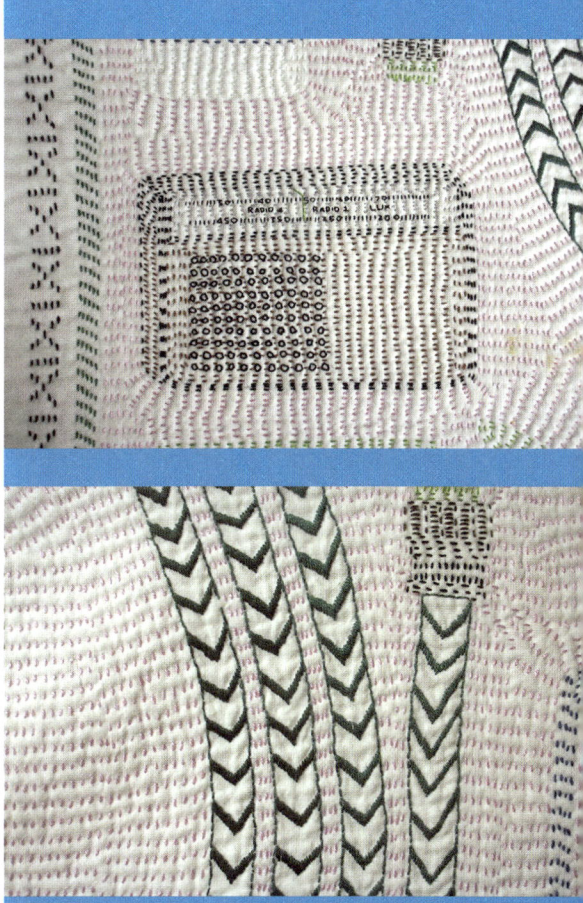

Details of Sewing Seed | Courtesy of The Whitworth Art Gallery | photo Michael Pollard

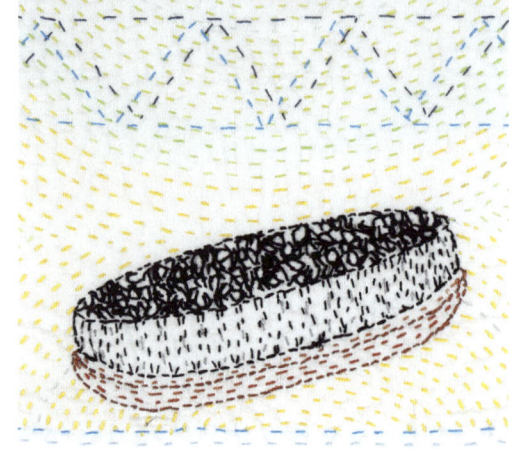
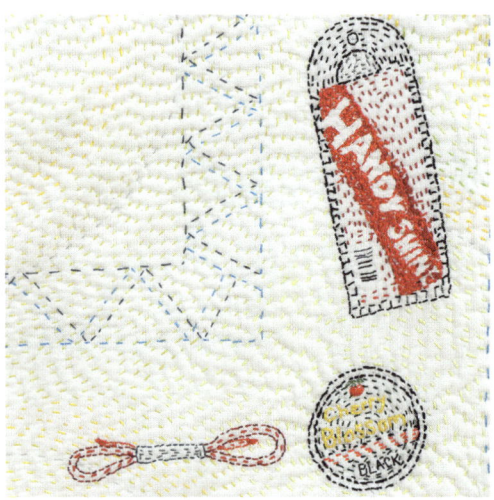
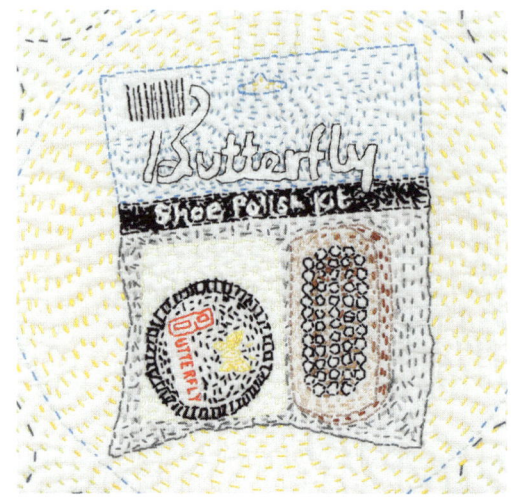

Shoeshine (2004–2024) | all photos David Bennett

Shoeshine (2004-24)

Shoeshine combines autobiography, popular culture, recycling and a celebration of the everyday. It commemorates shoe polishing, a small but overlooked ritual of life, and also the individuals who repair, clean and look after our shoes on the street, in shops, at airports and at stations. The piece draws on the phrase 'walk a mile in my shoes', asking us to imagine things from another person's point of view.

The quilt emerged after the discovery of an old wooden shoe brush and polish tin, part of a family's heritage, and the smell of the polish and the sight of these long-forgotten domestic objects brought back many childhood memories of the morning rituals involved in facing the world and going to school or work. Looking at the beautiful brush, I reflected on how this object, and many of the others in the tin, were now redundant in a world of canvas trainers; would a young person today even know what they were?

In documenting these everyday objects, Shoeshine not only casts light on the shoe repair shop, now less visible on our high streets

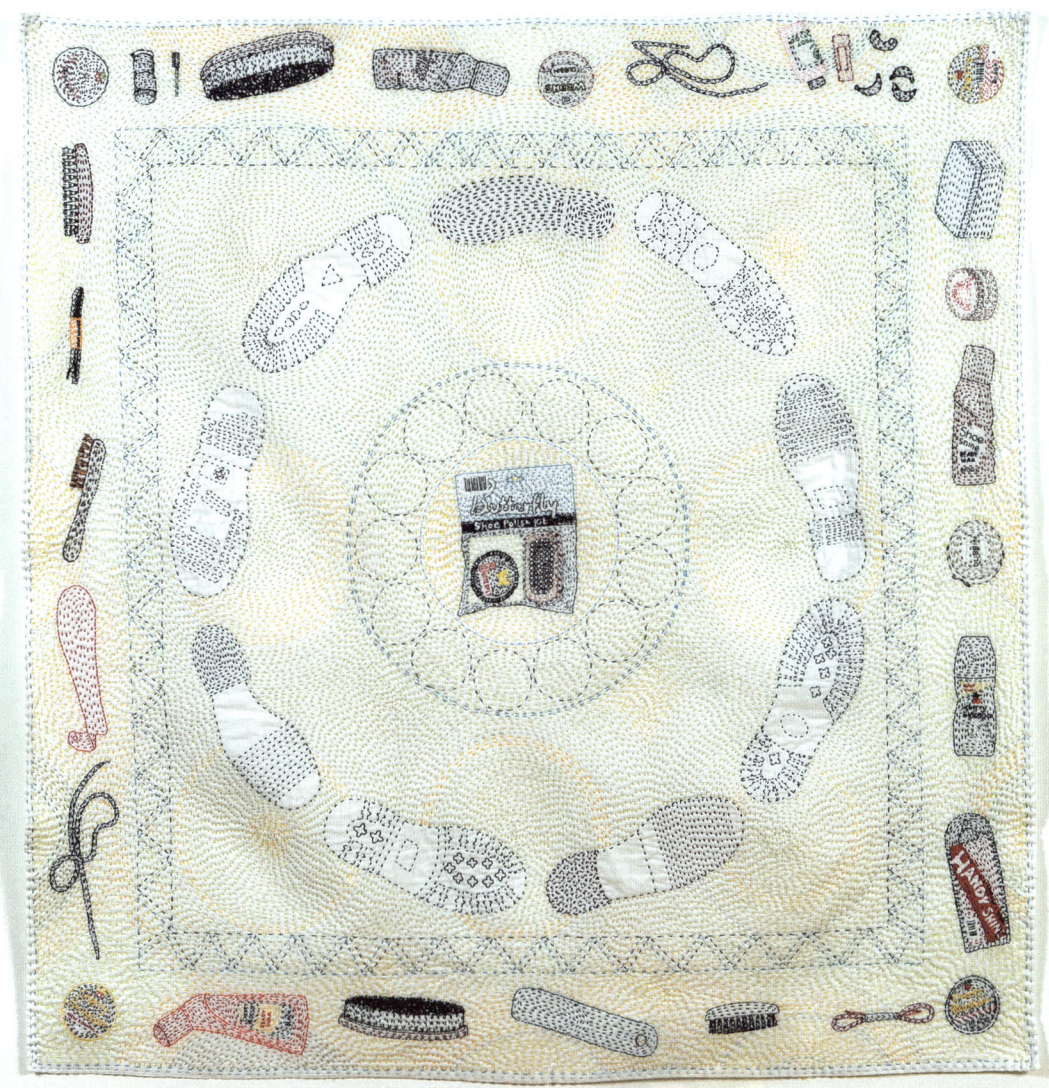

than in the past, it also acknowledges the significance of these objects in past daily lives and homes. The central image captures in stitch a modern shoe-cleaning kit surrounded by a circular pattern stitched to echo the shape of shoe polish tins. A larger circle made from the footprints of different shoes and resembling the instructions for a folk dance add to the composition and connect the cloth back to traditional kantha designs.

The cloth is framed by two borders, the outer one capturing in thread objects associated with shoe polishing and repair, the inner one circling around a stitched rendition of a shoe shine kit.

This quilt was created over a twenty-year period with some amendments made during the Covid pandemic lockdown – most notably a circular stitched pattern around the central motif and an extra border. These simple visual additions serve to divide the composition and draw the cloth together.

connecting threads

Identity and belonging

Threads of Identity, Burnage Academy for Boys (2016) | photo Mary Stark

connecting threads

Identity and Belonging

'Signatures are personal and physical inscriptions, symbolic and romantic gestures, but also visual signs that are still used today as "information" or "evidence" for verification of someone's identity'.

A Book of Signatures, *Harb and Edwardes 2010*

Folk art and textile history have intertwined throughout my practice for many years and text – a defining characteristic of folk and protest art – has always been a significant, recurring motif. In 2010, I was offered a Fellowship of the International Quilt Museum in the American city of Lincoln, Nebraska and was introduced to signature quilts, a genre of textiles I had never seen before. The experience heralded a new approach to making and an opportunity to raise awareness of this form of female endeavour on both sides of the Atlantic.

Signature quilts can be traced back to the 1830s. A form of tactile communication, each cloth (some of which are quilted and some of which are composed of just one layer – in Britain referred to as a coverlet) has surfaces filled with compositions made up of sewn signatures, all of which are worked by hand. Signature quilts were made to record friendships and family when settlers in the USA began moving west, leaving their groups and connections behind them. The cloths document the sewn autographs of loved ones and acted as comfort blankets and physical reminders. Over time their purpose and function changed and they developed as a type of fundraiser to raise money for good causes from, the local, such as new church building, or to national causes, including the war effort.

As with the Woven Air exhibition some twelve years earlier, seeing the US collection with its more than seventy quilts changed my direction overnight, triggering new trains of thought and opening ways of working with a whole range of communities. I relished the fact that these cloths and quilts were not just decorative items but also unique and valuable social history documents; each one a sensory record packed with stitched evidence. The signature, as motif and metaphor, works on so many levels. It is a recognised marker in Western society and most of the population know what it is and have one of their own. We need a signature as validation in many aspects of society, on a passport and many

Lincoln Nebraska, schools signature cloth workshop (2014) | photo Lynn Setterington

other documents; it is a tag used by graffiti artists to mark their territory and the celebrity signature is a marketing device to sell all kinds of products and services.

The wide variety of compositions and the accomplished stitching not only informed and guided my PhD, but it also led me to create twelve new artworks and projects between 2010–2017, as well as several exhibitions and an international partnership. (I returned to the International Quilt Museum in 2014 to showcase several collaborative quilts, alongside some of the historic American examples that had sparked this journey.)

I began to investigate how the theme could be developed and expanded in different settings. The fact that these cloths were a form of sensory petition was another positive aspect, linking the work to ideas around activism and political action. Seeing the North American examples reminded me of refugee families I knew back in Britain, people who had been forced to leave their families and connections behind in order to make a new life elsewhere.

Back in the UK, I used the discovery of the American museum's quilt collection as a catalyst to explore British examples held in archives around the country. My research uncovered a varied, rich, important but undervalued resource in both regional and national museums, as well as private collections. Historical examples I encountered ranged from the small-scale stitched handwriting of Lorina Bulwer (1838–1912), who in the late 19th century made long scroll-like embroideries describing her life in a workhouse in Norfolk, to the large political and trade union banners and activist artworks held in the People's History Museum in Manchester.

Signature cloths gained popularity in the UK in the 19th century. They were (and still are) made for a variety of reasons – some early examples pre-date the notion of crowd funding in that people donated money to causes and, in return, had their autographs

Gawthorpe Hall signature cloth (1905) Workpeople's Self-supporting Convalescent Homes Bazaar | photo Lynn Setterington

commemorated in thread. Many others, like their US counterparts, were made as fundraisers. These quilts were auctioned off or given as a raffle prize. One such example is a patriotic red, white and blue First World War quilt made in Coedpoeth, near Wrexham, North Wales. It contains the names of almost everyone in the village, from the butcher to members of the armed services, each one commemorated in thread. The cloth was owned by a woman whose grandfather had won it in a raffle and she subsequently donated it to Wrexham Museum so that would stay close to the community that it represents.

A substantial number of signature quilts have come to light in Britain over the years, sparking the interest of academics in a range of disciplines. There are many examples on public display, including in the community hall in Sturminster Newton, Dorset; Robin Hood's Bay Museum, North Yorkshire and Bankfield Museum in Halifax.

One interesting example is in Oldham Museum. It is not dated and the name of the maker(s) is hidden amongst a mass of autographs worked in a spiral on the fabric. Often in folk art the maker is unknown and despite all the signatures, many of these cloths follow this unwritten rule. Some are the work of one individual, but more common is a shared effort with multiple identities on show. As Maria Elena Buszek suggests in her book *Extra/Ordinary: Craft and Contemporary Art* (Duke University Press, 2012) popular and folk art offer 'a means of communicating beyond an elite community and letting the real world back into art.'

The originators of the cloth in Oldham Museum are sewn boldly into its surface, the Townswomen's Guild. This is a national women's friendly association still in operation today and dating back to 1929. It is similar in its aim to the Women's Institute, to bring women together to educate, work together and offer support for good causes.

The design for this cloth is unusual in that the sewn signatures, each worked in a different coloured thread, curve around the motif of the Townswomen's Guild in a spiral. The orientation is not fixed, maybe because it is a tablecloth and would be displayed flat and, by working the signatures in the round, no one person can be singled out as the ringleader or key agitator.

Sreepur Quilt (2012) | photo Mary Stark

Sreepur Quilt (2012)

The Sreepur Quilt was a partnership project with Sreepur Village charity, a community located forty miles from Dhaka in rural Bangladesh. The Sreepur Village charity was established thirty-five years ago and it runs and funds the village, working with mothers and children for up to three years to increase their chances of remaining together. It offers many resources including shelter, food, nutrition, education, health care, life skills training, child safeguarding and protection, and social reintegration.

This collaborative quilt brought together two themes – kanthas and signature cloths/quilts. I worked on the project at a distance, involving the Sreepur women as participants and the outcome functions both as a record of those involved in Sreepur in 2011 and as a sensory vehicle to raise awareness of the work of this important charity.

The project developed in 2011 following Threading Dreams, an exhibition in Gallery Oldham, which showcased contemporary kanthas, some of which had been made in Sreepur while others were my own kantha-based work. It was a joint venture with Ruby Porter, a Sreepur trustee. Ruby, a former primary school teacher from Liverpool, visited the village regularly to work with the women there, developing their craft and textile skills. When Ruby and I met in Oldham to plan the Threading Dreams exhibition, my signature cloth research

connecting threads

Sreepur women (2012), Sami, Tia, Rya, Ismat, Maya and Ruby Porter
photo Sreepur charity

was just beginning, and Ruby suggested another, different joint venture with Sreepur. She offered to discuss the idea with the women in Bangladesh and provide cloth for their individual autographs. She also agreed to post the completed signatures back to the UK so that the names could be joined together to create a quilt.

Once the idea had been agreed with the women, Sreepur provided an ivory silk cloth for the sewn signatures. Using such a luxurious fabric, Ruby suggested, would instil a sense of worth into the work and help the women feel valued. No guidance was given on how to create the sewn signatures, rather the women were encouraged to use their individual embroidery skills, so the project developed organically. After several weeks, parcels of stitched names began to arrive. Alongside their own autographs, the women had created stitched markers of the Sreepur Trustees,

embroidering their names in both English and Bengali and adding embroidered flowers, figures and patterns into the cloths. The sewn autographs varied in style and stitch processes and ranged from the simple and direct to the elaborate and complex. On seeing all these sewn signatures, I decided to create a quilt drawing on my ongoing research and knowledge of signature cloths.

Sreepur Quilt detail (2012) | photo Mary Stark

Edge detail of Sreepur Quilt (2012) |photo Mary Stark

One issue I had not foreseen, was that all the names were stitched on slightly different sizes of cloth. As the stitching often encroached on the edges, it was not possible to standardise the dimensions of each cloth. However, once all the pieces were together, we were able to lay them out and devise a plan to unite them. There were thirty-seven contributions in all, each one showing individual skill and ingenuity. The weight of expectation was heavy – how could they be brought together in a way that celebrated shared creativity? Looking at the names on each cloth, the task felt both a privilege and a huge responsibility.
The solution, as is often the case, came from a reliable and valuable resource; historic textiles.

During my continuing research into signature cloths, I had uncovered many ingenious examples in British museums and private collections. The compositions created and good causes supported varied, as did the locations where the cloths were housed, but the one that resonated most clearly with the Sreepur project lay in the textile archive at Gawthorpe Hall in Lancashire. It was a cloth rather than a quilt, made in 1905 as a fundraiser for the Workpeople's Self-supporting Convalescent Homes Bazaar. Research with Alison Slater, an MMU colleague, revealed that this organisation, a precursor of the National Health Service, enabled workers to be cared for in a rest home if they became ill.

The Gawthorpe coverlet is made from cut squares of fabric, each containing five to six sewn signatures. These individual square blocks are joined together with lace to make a grid. It is a good example of a pragmatic solution to the problem of group work; it is difficult for several people to work on a large piece of cloth simultaneously as everyone needs to hold the material and turn it as they sew. We decided to adapt the technique for the 2011 Sreepur cloth.

connecting threads

Sreepur Quilt (2012) | photo Mary Stark

Remembering Emily (2013)

Remembering Emily explored feminist history, community action and gender equality using the signature cloth to celebrate the life of Suffragette, Emily Wilding Davison (1872–1913). Davison died on 8 June, 1913, when she fell under King George V's horse at the Epsom Derby. Whether she intended to kill herself is open to debate – current thinking is that her aim was to pin a Suffragette rosette on the King's horse and was accidently killed in the process.

2013 marked the centenary of Davison's death. Searching the archives at The Women's Library in London (now held at the London School of Economics), I discovered handwritten letters, including Davison's signature and the train ticket from the day of her death. These offered poignant reminders of her fate and material evidence of how much life has changed in the last century.

However, while the Gawthorpe coverlet was orderly and uniform in its design, thanks to the standard size of the signature squares, the Sreepur blocks were irregular shapes and varied in size. We decided to celebrate this fact and join the signatures together with a mix of old and new lace. This decorative feature not only brought something different to the signature cloth genre, it also helped to fuse contemporary and historical signature quilt research.

A final element united the Sreepur signatures with their Bangladeshi heritage when a utilitarian kantha, a gift from a textile student with family in Bangladesh, was added under the silk and lace structure. The weight and solidity of this modern cloth helped to support the delicate fabrics, adding strength to the textile's structure and also grounded the quilt back in its home country.

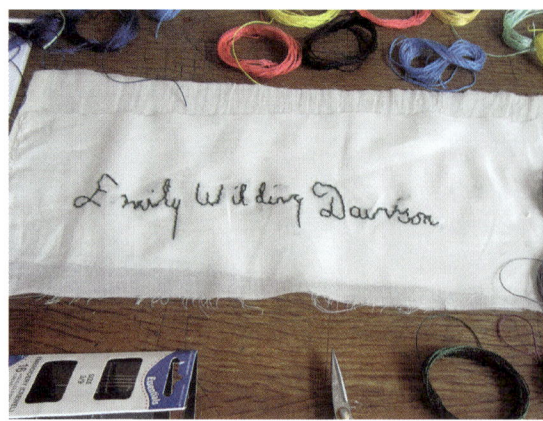
Sewing Emily's signature | photo Lynn Setterington

Remembering Emily workshop MMU staff and students (2013) | photo Lynn Setterington

In April 2013, the 100 Deeds Project (Davison's epitaph being 'Deeds not Words'), offered an opportunity to celebrate this remarkable woman and the centenary of her death. It was an online project in which the public were encouraged to share contributions of good deeds on the website with the aim of collecting one hundred good acts. By April, the submissions included simple acts of remembrance, such as the reading of a feminist narrative to a daughter, or leading a walk in her memory.

The timing of the anniversary coincided with the opening of a new art school building at Manchester Metropolitan University. I saw an opportunity to bring staff and students together on campus to remember Davison, drawing on my archive research and the notion of sewn signatures. The plan for our contribution was simple: to commemorate this important figure through the creation of a stitched petition made up of one hundred sewn autographs.

In early May, two Remembering Emily workshop dates were shared across MMU, inviting anyone interested in the project to come along, stitch their autograph, connect with others and add to the shared artwork. An online Eventbrite sign-up ensured that the workspace was not too overcrowded and there was enough material for each participant. Students from different faculties joined in, as did academics and administrative staff and, as with earlier projects, the sewing event provided an opportunity to share knowledge in an informal way. Sewing skills were not taught at the sessions – stitching autographs, much like a written signature, was left open to personal invention and interpretation. However, simple diagrams of linear stitches were available if people required some guidance.

Cloth, threads, scissors, needles and drawing equipment were provided for testing and sampling ideas, along with some visual

connecting threads

Remembering Emily workshop MMU staff and students (2013)
photo Lynn Setterington

information and literature on the history of signature cloths. I chose cotton voile as a ground – a light, fine cloth rather than the heavy cottons usually used as grounds for traditional signature cloths. To make joining the autographs together straightforward and ensure that the final work was aesthetically coherent, participants were asked to stitch on rectangles measuring 30×10cm.

On the day of the workshops, (two half-day sessions) we showed clips from Andrew Marr's *History of Britain* film of the fateful day in 1913 and Davison's funeral procession. We also shared information about the 100 Deeds project, so everyone could see what had been completed so far and add more if they wished. Sarah Evans, one of the 100 Deeds project organisers, also joined us in one of the stitch workshops. There was plenty of discussion during the day too, ranging from everyday gossip and textile-specific queries to politics and whether there is now less political art being discussed or made at universities.

One thing I had not anticipated were requests for involvement in the creative process by people who could not attend the workshop in person. It was not possible to offer additional workshops, so we came up with the idea of creating a simple kit made up of a piece of cotton voile, sewing thread and basic instructions which we posted, or gave out to, new participants. Despite the guidelines, some of these additional autographs came back to us sewn not on the cotton voile but on a mix of white cotton cloths. That is the reality of co-operative working in practice.

Once all the donations were complete, Emily Wilding Davison's own sewn signature was added, making her presence felt and connecting her to a new generation of supporters. With only a two-week turnaround to the centenary of her death, we needed to a find a simple way of uniting the hundred autographs. The solution was to machine stitch them together in a long, narrow sewn petition, measuring approximately 10m long, leaving the edges of each cloth raw. This accelerated the final making-up process and circumvented the onerous task of hemming a hundred pieces of cloth.

As with all projects, there are lessons learned along the way and, having taken time to evaluate and reflect, it is clear that using a non-fray fabric for the signatures would have

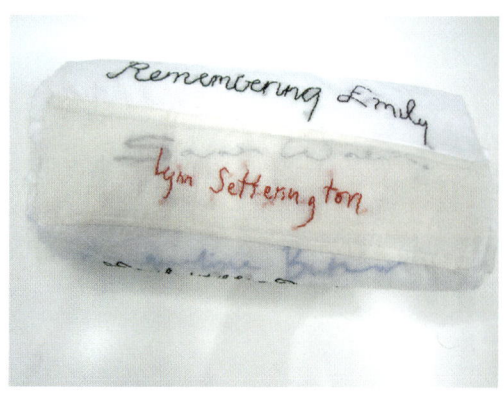

Remembering Emily laid out (2013) | photo Lynn Setterington

left: **Remembering Emily rolled up (2013)** | photo Lynn Setterington

connecting threads

The procession at the Wilding Festival, London with Remembering Emily (2013) | photo Sarah Evans

resulted in a more visually pleasing solution. Nevertheless, using the cotton voile brought its own benefits. This light, delicate material contributed an alternative quality to the signature cloth and ensured the signatures could be rolled into a compact bundle that was easy to transport.

Like the other co-created stitch projects I have worked on, Remembering Emily's impact extended far beyond one collaborative cloth. What began as a response to an online submission developed into a university partnership and haptic commemoration of a feminist icon, drawing together past and present histories in a thread petition. The project received national recognition when BBC Radio 4 featured it on Woman's Hour. Several students involved in the making were interviewed and so this important object, Emily Wilding Davison's anniversary and her legacy came to the attention of new audiences.

The scroll was also displayed at the People's History Museum, Manchester, and at MMU during an open day, winning a knowledge exchange award. Remembering Emily's final

Detail of sewn signatures including Sam Orton | photo Lynn Setterington

outing was in London at the Wilding Festival at St George's, Bloomsbury on Saturday 15 June, when Davison's great niece touchingly placed the scroll on the spot where her ancestor's coffin had lain one hundred years earlier.

This project also helped raise awareness of other Suffragette testaments involving the sewn signature. One example features the embroidered autographs of Suffragettes incarcerated in Holloway Prison in 1909. They were memorialised in a banner designed by Ann Macbeth (1875–1948), which is now held in The Museum of London's collection. Other hand-sewn autographs include the Suffragette Handkerchief displayed at the Priest House in Hoathly, West Sussex and one sewn by the militant Suffragette and holder of the Women's Social and Political Union Hunger Strike medal, Janie Terrero. Both are the subject of academic research, the former by Denise Jones and the latter by Maureen Daly Goggin.

Ten years on, reflecting on our shared endeavour and looking once again at the varied embroidered surfaces, this narrow cloth provides a wealth of sensory information. Each autograph is a unique record, detailing each of the makers. Some are highly accomplished and technically proficient; others are made by less experienced hands, possibly those new to sewing, and one autograph remains unfinished, reflecting the uncertainties in shared making and our different levels of commitment.

Looking back over these markers of identity is a poignant reminder of the passage of time, given that many of the people involved in Remembering Emily have moved on from Manchester and at least one person who contributed to the cloth in 2013 is no longer with us.

Designs for two tote bags made from found materials | photo David Bennett

Signature Bags (2011)

This collection of handmade tote bags was created in 2011 with Katab, a group of textile artisans living in Ahmedabad, India. Originally from rural Gujarat, this group had, like many others, moved to the city for economic reasons. The idea for these bags built on an earlier, 2007 project in when I had worked with the women in Ahmedabad to try and increase the market for the items these skilled makers produced. The 2007 collaboration resulted in a range of tote bags featuring a hand-appliqued slogan in either English or Gujarati. The design had originated from a simple collage created from Indian newspapers (a direct way to use a cheap and plentiful material during the design process).

The bags themselves were made from khadi cloth, a traditional hand-spun, handwoven fabric well known in India and famously advocated by Mahatma Gandhi as a cloth

Tote bag made by Katab group from khadi cloth (2007) | photo David Bennett

of the people. The design was simple and could be adapted and reconfigured easily, and the women used their textile skills to re-imagine the design using a variety of colourways and text. The results were bold, vibrant and fun, although not always predictable.

Unfortunately, feedback from one of the Indian partner organisations suggested that handmade was not a selling feature for Indian consumers, because, unlike in the UK where the term can attract a premium, handmade items are commonplace in India. Nevertheless, we decided to carry on with the partnership and sell the bags in small independent shops in Britain instead, returning the profits to the women who made them.

In 2011, I began working with the Katab group again, this time at a distance. The project was facilitated in Ahmedabad by Lokesh Ghai, a textile scholar who knew the group and proved to be a vital link. In this partnership, I was mindful that such artisans often remain invisible and uncredited for their skilled work, so we decided to make new tote bags using a simple appliqué design that foregrounded the women themselves by using their first names as the main decorative feature on the bag. This approach acknowledged and celebrated the women's contribution as creators and was a small step in highlighting their community. It also resonated strongly with the exploration of sewn autographs as a marker of identity and my continuing focus in my own practice on a celebration of the everyday and overlooked.

Detail of Jalpa Ben signature tote bag (2011)
photo Mary Stark

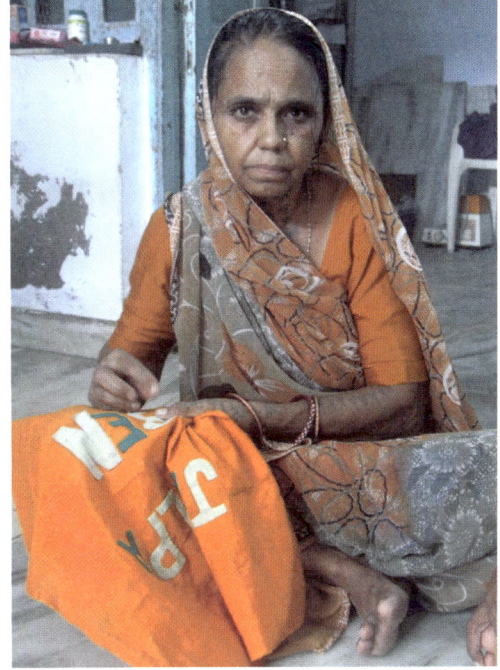

Jalpa Ben (2011) | photo Lokesh Ghai

connecting threads

Twelve signature bags made by Katab (2011) | photo Mary Stark

Lokesh took the idea of using names to the group and they approved, again using khadi cloth to make and decorate their own signature bags. As with the earlier iteration of this project, some women chose to write in Gujarati and some in English. (The word 'Ben' seen after many of the first names on the bags is similar to the term 'auntie' in Britain and suggests not necessarily a blood relative but a revered elder in the community.) The resulting bags were shown in exhibitions in the UK to promote the group's identity and their skilled work.

Threads of Identity banner (2016) | photo Mary Stark

Threads of Identity (2016)

Threads of Identity marked the 30th anniversary of the death of Ahmed Iqbal Ullah, a young boy killed in 1986 in a racially motivated crime at a south Manchester school. The project's aim was to raise awareness of Ullah's life, share his story and explore issues of young male identity, race and stereotypes about embroidery using sewn and drawn signatures as a marker of personal identity. It was a partnership with the Ahmed Iqbal Ullah Race Relations Archive (www.racearchive.org.uk) and fifteen pupils in Burnage Academy for Boys, the state secondary school Ullah attended. The Trust is an open access resource named in memory of Ullah, based in Manchester Central Library.

Working with a group of young boys was a new venture for me and a very different undertaking to previous signature cloth work which had focused mostly on work with adult women. However, a creative mindset, flexible approach and a supportive team with knowledge of the benefits and tensions in this way of working to assist in running the sessions helped me to navigate this uncertain terrain. Not thinking too far ahead and taking stock, one week at a time, was an important first step. This incremental approach was useful in allowing us to see and understand how the boys responded and reacted to the creative sessions and also to accommodate different skill levels, something which is particularly important

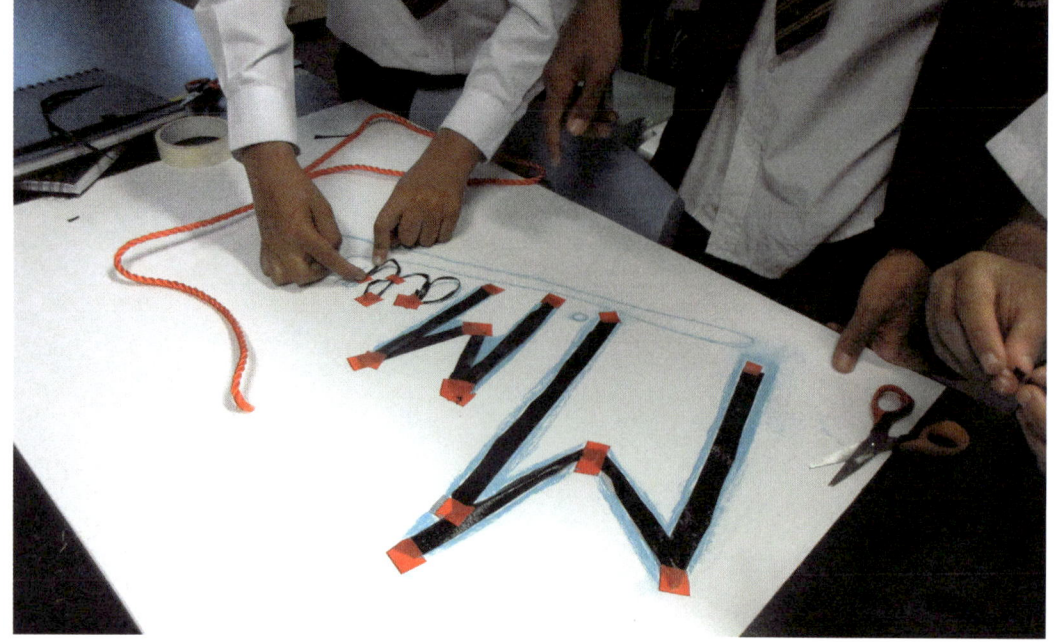

Drawing workshops with Burnage Boys (2016) | photo: Lynn Setterington

when participants are unfamiliar with stitching. The boys came with different abilities, some had some prior experience of hand sewing but others had none at all. Likewise, a few were confident in creative methods while some struggled with these new concepts.

Threads of Identity evolved through defined but separate stages. It began with a group visual discussion and handling session to help the boys understand and appreciate both the feel and potential of a signature cloth. Images of different types and styles of signature cloths were shared in a visual presentation alongside physical examples of traditional hand-sewn, laser cut and digitally stitched autograph cloths. Debate followed about the signature as used today as a form of personal identity, the role of graffiti and signing documents. Each boy was asked to collect ten drawn signatures of people in their lives. One unforeseen hurdle that may have impacted on this stage of the project was that the education officer at the Race Archive moved to another post. He was of Bangladeshi origin and male so might have provided a link between the artist and boys. However, again, there was not time in the schedule to wait for a new appointment and so the work progressed. Thankfully, the head of Art in the school was a positive addition, knew the boys and was interested in how the project's aim linked to her own background in textile design. They were also all given a personal sketch book to foster creative thinking and play. Work began on the practical aspects of the project incrementally, first testing different ways to create personal signature drawings using different materials including braid, string and pens on paper, then moving to large-scale signatures made in the school corridors using thick tape.

These activities functioned as ice breakers and the boys responded well, firstly working alone and then in small groups. The next phase involved sewing, but again it started slowly, exploring simple techniques such as threading a needle and tying a knot. A plain white handkerchief was given to each boy

connecting threads

for testing and sampling and provided a standard size to work into. (Unlike Remembering Emily, these units were hemmed and edged.) Using a plentiful, relatively cheap and easily found material source was a good strategy as it meant we could take risks with the sampling, knowing more supplies were available. Alongside these sensory activities, the boys started to draw and test the arrangements of their collected signatures with the help of students from MMU who came and worked with the group to support learning and share creative skills.

The name of the school, 'Burnage Academy for Boys' was brought into the frame at this stage to focus the design process, as we had noticed in the drawing stage that the boys' ten signatures were randomly configured without any unity or purpose. It was obvious that leaving this design element completely

Workshop sewing signatures, Burnage Academy for Boys (2016) | photo Mary Stark

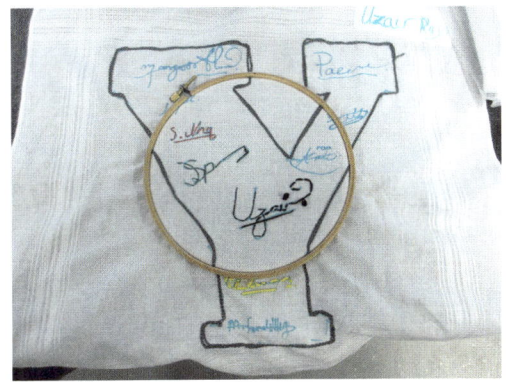

Composition of collected signatures (2016)
photo Mary Stark

open was too much of a challenge for this young age group and that more direction was needed. Allocating a sewn letter (and one number) from 'Burnage Academy 4 Boys' to each of the participants, which gave the boys an individual framework that helped them to arrange their autographs in a more cohesive way. The letters were sewn onto the handkerchiefs using coloured threads and a Cornelly machine, which creates a chain stitch. This was a relatively quick, simple and effective way of adding a focus to the work and grouping the autographs.

A charged moment in the project came with the discovery of Ullah's own autograph in one of his diaries from the 1980s. This not only brought the past pupil into view, it also

The boys design the signature layout in a sketchbook (2016) | photo Mary Stark

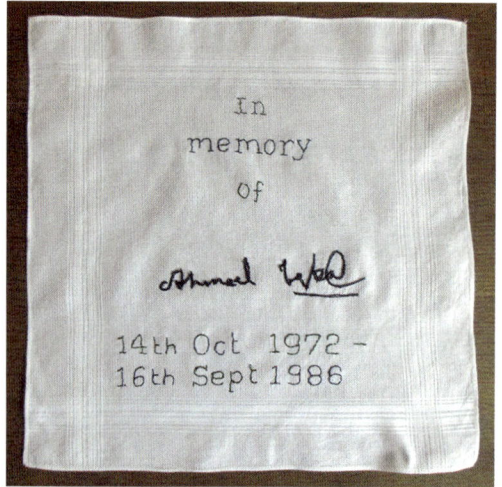

Handkerchief sewn in memory of Ahmed Iqbal (2016) | photo Lynn Setterington

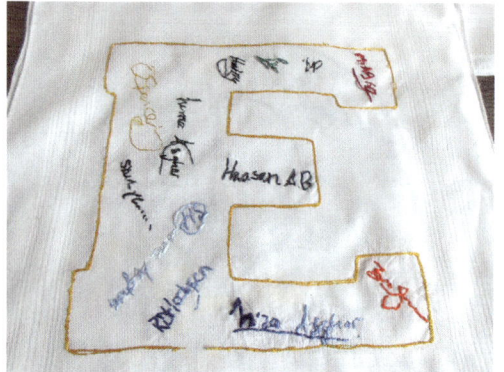

Sewing signatures onto handkerchiefs, Burnage Academy for Boys (2016) | photo Lynn Setterington

enabled his signature to be worked into the cloth, connecting past and current Burnage boys. (Something which resonated with Remembering Emily.)

The final stage of making was to join the handkerchiefs together. To bring something different to the contemporary signature cloth and retain a trace of the handkerchiefs, the white cotton squares were united with an insertion stitch created on a faggoting machine. This was an effective and different method of joining a signature cloth, uniting the squares while retaining the light, sheer quality of the handkerchiefs.

As with other complex projects there were unexpected outcomes in Threads of Identity. An important element that was not scheduled in the initial planning was the making of a short film of the shared making. Money had been allocated in the budget for photographic documentation but on reflection it seemed more valuable to include a specialist film maker to record moving images and produce a short film that could showcase to different audiences. As a result, Mary Stark was added to the team, and she subsequently filmed some of the creative sessions and the celebration event to detail some of the key stages of the project (available on vimeo).

Three Manchester Textile in Practice undergraduates also worked on the project and their input was important, both encouraging the creative work and fostering dialogue and exchange. One student was from Northern Ireland, one from a Bangladeshi background and one who had roots in the north of England. Each talked about their home life, hobbies and aspirations. The one from Northern Ireland talked about Gaelic football and hockey, which were new topics for the boys. A visit to Manchester School of Art was planned to see the students' work and the facilities on offer and this was delayed so as to coincide with a first screening of the film, a positive way to end the project and share the first viewing together. This visit was valuable as it allowed the boys to experience an art school environment for the first time, to see

Joining the handkerchiefs together on the faggoter machine | photo Mary Stark

workshops in action and understand how a creative degree can unfold.

Reflecting on the impact of Threads of Identity eight years on, there were other benefits alongside the legacy of the cloth and film. Firstly, connections have remained in place and the boys from Burnage Academy visit the art school degree shows regularly. It is testament to the project that all the boys contributed to the final cloth and several talked in the film about their increased confidence, new skills and abilities.

Significantly, the artwork has been on display in Burnage School ever since it was made, provoking debate and discussion with the teachers and visibly highlighting that boys can sew creatively.

The 2016 Casey Review into opportunity and integration in our most isolated and deprived communities confirmed the low rates of social mobility amongst Bangladeshi and Pakistani ethnic groups, who made up most of the participants in Threads of Identity. Dame Louise Casey also suggested in the review that working with schools and local communities to promote opportunities for pupils to mix with others from different backgrounds is a way forward (2016: 17). Given that the key partners in Threads of Identity were a charity promoting and encouraging good race relations and a high school in a Manchester suburb serving boys from a predominantly working-class Asian Muslim population, this project bridged some of these invisible boundaries that, albeit unintentionally, develop between communities and institutions.

connecting threads

Watercolour drawing for Sew Near – Sew Far
photo Lynn Setterington

Testing materials and threads for sewn signatures (2017) | photo Lynn Setterington

Sew Near – Sew Far (2017)

Sew Near – Sew Far took the signature cloth in a new and different direction, re-presenting the Brontë sisters' pseudonymous signatures on a vast scale on the moors of Haworth, the place that inspired much of their creativity. It was a commission for the Brontë Parsonage Museum and Meeting Point 2, an innovative approach bringing artists and museums together to look afresh at history. Meeting Point is a series of UK-based partnerships devised by the organisation Arts and Heritage. The aim is to forge links between museums, archives and heritage settings and contemporary artists through commissions and are funded by the Arts Council.

Like many of the creative interventions described in this book, Sew Near was rooted in archival and stitch-based research. In this instance, the starting point was a small piece of paper containing three tiny, ink-drawn autographs of Acton, Currer and Ellis Bell I came across at the Brontë Parsonage

Sew Near – Sew Far on Haworth moor (2017) | photo Lunar Al

Museum. These pseudonymous male signatures, created by the three Brontë sisters, offered a real connection to the siblings and I was struck by the contrast between their handmade delicacy and the bleak, open moors around Haworth. The idea of melding the two together was the catalyst for the creation of a piece of land-based art.

The aim was to recreate the three Bell signatures on a monumental scale on the hills above Haworth, moving the signature cloth away from its domestic roots and into the outdoors to look afresh at the sisters' legacy away from the confines of the Parsonage. The linear forms would contain autographs within autographs, made up of sewn contributions by both local people and Brontë fans who would donate them in a series of creative workshops.

Having secured the commission, the first step was to find a location for the transitory work, then test suitable materials that could

connecting threads

withstand the exposed and unpredictable conditions of the moors. This new way of working exposed a whole different set of hurdles in collaborative making. First and foremost was finding out who owned the land in and around Haworth and ascertaining whether the owners would be willing to let us borrow it for a few weeks to install the work. Fortunately, a small, local organisation linked to Haworth Young Farmers called Fields of Vision came on board. Andrew Wood and Joe Holmes had invaluable knowledge of both the people and landscape in this area and were enormously helpful in navigating the varied local issues. After several recce trips and much discussion, we settled on a location three miles from the town, and close to the Brontë waterfalls. Not only were the fields there open and free from trees and other obstructions, but the sites could also be seen from the Brontë Way, a popular tourist hiking trail. The land itself (owned by Yorkshire Water) was leased to a sheep and cattle farmer who Fields of Vision thought would be open to working with us.

Next came visits to fabric suppliers, builders' merchants and hardware shops to look for suitable outdoor materials to create the linear artwork. We settled on debris netting, a knitted fabric used on building sites to prevent debris falling. Cheap, plentiful, suitable for the outdoors and available in many colours, it was ideal. The size of the work also meant that we also had to ensure that the signatures could be seen. Traditional embroidery threads were not robust enough so we tested thicker yarns not embroidery threads but wool and string mixes, eventually settling on range of different threads including knitting wools, string and dishcloth cottons.

From the start, the aim of Sew Near was to work with local groups unfamiliar with the Brontë narrative as a way of increasing awareness of the sisters' legacy and sharing the local women's achievements with different organisations in Yorkshire. Talk English, a charity that teaches English in creative ways, was an obvious partner and, following a visit to the group at its base in Bradford and discussions with a tutor, it joined the project. Workshops in two venues in Bradford provided a consistent point of contact and a way to collect drawn and sewn signatures, while at the same time allowing us to explore the Brontë sisters' work and life stories together. As well as these workshops, we also ran several open stitch sessions in and around Haworth so that local people and visitors to the museum could be included in the donation process. These were purposefully open sessions so anyone passing by could join in and were more about creative inclusion and making your mark than good sewing skills.

Once again, building a team of trusted and reliable individuals as part of the project was a crucial element in Sew Near. This not only helped to navigate the uncertainties of such a complex undertaking, it also allowed joint discussions to take place and meant the weight of responsibility did not fall entirely on one person's shoulders. The team included Lauren Livesey and Jenna Holmes from the Brontë Parsonage Museum; members of Arts and Heritage, which facilitated the commission and publicity for the project; Andrew Wood and Joe Holmes who were the mainstay of Fields of Vision and whose local knowledge and expertise smoothed the way in this challenging new arena and Lunar AI whose breath-taking aerial shots of the signatures on the moors were instrumental in the short film documenting the project. Design students from MMU were a crucial element too, helping not just in the workshops but also with prototyping ideas and offering hands-on support.

The decision to use white, rather than coloured, net for the signatures had more to do with the visibility of the white cloth than anything else, but it added another dimension to the piece. The linear form of the work echoes ancient chalk monuments carved in the British landscape such as the Cerne Abbas Giant and Wiltshire's white horses and the signatures help us to consider these icons through a female lens.

Being outdoors brought new challenges – not least the changeable weather and uncertain conditions when installing the work. For example, we had to ensure that the

Jayne Eyre sewing her signature (2017)
photo Lynn Setterington

Visitors from Illinois on a literary tour of Britian (2017) | photo Lynn Setterington

Talk English workshop, Bradford (2017)
photo Lynn Setterington

Lynn Setterington installing Sew Near with (r-l) Lauren Livesey, Joe Holmes, Andrew Wood and Peter Spence (2017) | photo Jonathan Turner

signatures could be read from the viewing place on the Brontë Way and that the perspective was right. Thankfully, working with Fields of Vision was smooth and productive and, with walkie talkies and lots of shouting (there was no mobile signal on the moors), we managed to position the three signatures in place in a single day. We also had to find a way to transport the artwork and buckets of nails (needed to fix the linear structures) across the moors without vehicle access. Fortunately, Andrew and Joe came to the rescue again with their local knowledge and an off-road vehicle. Booking a drone company to document the work from the air was another new venture for me. The final surprise came when the signatures were removed from the hillside and we discovered animal teeth marks – probably cattle, foxes or badgers – in the white net and some of the sewn autographs.

The fact that the Brontë sisters are international literary icons shifted the focus of Sew Near away from my usual territory of untold narratives – although the sisters' early death, their lack of status as unmarried women and Yorkshire roots all resonated. Working on the signatures meant that we were able to experience Brontë fandom – an international phenomenon – at first hand. Signposts on the Brontë Way are written in English and Japanese, the museum and Haworth draw visitors from across the world

connecting threads

150 sewn signatures removed from the moors (2017) | photo Lynn Setterington

and our stitch workshops were attended by – amongst others – Jayne Eyre from Yorkshire, two friends from Illinois on a literary tour of Britain and even Brontë the dog. An unforeseen challenge of working in an outdoor tourist destination was assessing visitor numbers. With people arriving from different directions, it was simply not feasible to ascertain actual figures. However the upside was that anyone, whether out for a stroll with the dog, hiking the Brontë Way or fell running, could see and explore the work. The short film, which captured key elements of the project, was also shared on the Brontë Parsonage website (www.bronte.org.uk) providing an additional accessible strand to the project and a way to share the work globally.

A number of those involved in creating the sewn signatures came to the launch event, though many of the Asian families could not come on a Saturday due to family commitments. However, we had several emails and letters of thanks acknowledging the value of being involved. The Talk English tutor commented:

'The project allowed the Talk English learners… to explore the rich heritage of the Brontë Sisters and to integrate with other communities and allowed them to discover Haworth and the Parsonage for the first time, despite them living in Bradford.'

Other participants commented:
'On behalf of C and myself as her Nana, I would like to thank you for giving her the chance to be part of your Brontë project. C thoroughly enjoyed taking part and was so proud on Sunday when we visited the moor to see the finished work in situ, we managed to find C's contribution straight away which was a bonus.'

Walkers looking at the signatures within signatures (2017) | photo Jonathan Turner

Talk to an English group on a visit to Haworth (2017) | photo Lynn Setterington

'My sister and I are so grateful for these amazing pictures. The signatures engraved on the Yorkshire hills with fabric and yarn are simply amazing. I love that the heather was out – the hills were glorious as a background to the signatures. Congratulations, Lynn – and thank you for letting us be a part of this.'

Judith King, a Director of Arts and Heritage commented, 'the Meeting Point 2 commission for the Parsonage Museum is brilliant, and I know that everyone is so pleased with it. Sew Near – Sew Far addressed the brief exceptionally well.'

Sew Near – Sew Far's novel outcome not only took the signature cloth into new terrain, but by placing the pseudonymous signatures outside of the museum, the work united the sisters and reconnected them with the moors of West Yorkshire. The project was also significant in highlighting the poor visibility of female authors of the 19th century and drawing attention to the under-representation of women that continues to this day. This project brings together different disciplines through a creative framework, drawing on geography, English literature, history, socially engaged art, feminist theory, museology, land art pedagogy and, of course, embroidery practice, providing an innovative approach towards decolonising museums.

Visitors exploring the signatures on Haworth Moors (2017) | photo Jonathan Turner

Blue Plaques

The Bradford workshops were devised on the assumption that each session would attract a different cohort of people. As it turned out however, we had a regular group of women who turned up each week. They sewed their names in week one, so we needed to come up with another project. The idea we suggested was to embroider commemorative blue plaques – a creative topic that opened up new ways of exploring British culture and history and importantly, given we needed

connecting threads

to start immediately, had already been tested. It linked neatly to the main project too as there are blue plaques to Charlotte and Anne Brontë in Manchester and Scarborough. This approach also provided a way of getting to know the women as we discussed who they wished to commemorate and why. Most women embroidered plaques for a family member and the most poignant and impactful outcome was the one designed by a widow in memory of her late husband who had been killed in Syria.

This additional, unexpected project raised different tensions, chiefly working out what to do with the resulting plaques. There was not much time for discussion or planning and, in hindsight, it would have helped to bring in an archivist to explain the concept as a history project and someone else to organise a public display. Attempts to show the plaques in a venue in Bradford proved unsuccessful and so, although the plaques were completed on time, the outcomes remained unseen.

connecting threads

Health and Wellbeing

Cross stitch sampler (2021) | photo Lynn Setterington

connecting threads

Health and Wellbeing

s we move towards the second quarter of the 21st century, health and wellbeing have become major preoccupations. From National Health Service waiting lists to the huge rise in anxiety and poor mental health in young people, this topic is increasingly in the headlines and presenting new challenges in all our lives. The All Party, Creative Health Review (2023) acknowledges the value of creative work, arguing that these activities are fundamental to our health and wellbeing, and provides evidence that engaging with creativity and culture has a positive impact on both. The accessibility, availability and scope of creative work mean that its worth is becoming more widely known and valued and the three projects featured in this section put the concept into practice in different ways. Two were collaborative, the third an individual response to Covid-19.

Hand stitch has become far more recognised as a narrative device used by many people to tell their stories. This includes many on the margins of society whose names would not have been known had they not taken to working with a needle and thread.

One of these marginal people is Mary Frances Heaton (1801-1878). A music teacher in her thirties, Mary was incarcerated in Stanley Royd, the West Riding pauper lunatic asylum, in 1837 after causing a disturbance in the local church. She remained there for the next thirty-six years when she was transferred to another asylum where she died aged 78. Throughout her imprisonment, Mary embroidered samplers voicing her protests about the judgements made against her. These are important documents, a rare legacy of one of the unfortunate individuals incarcerated in a Victorian asylum. (Her work is archived at the Mental Health Museum, Wakefield.)

Meanwhile, on the other side of the Atlantic in New Mexico, Policarpio Valencia (1854-1931) stitched his diaries onto woven blankets formed from layers and layers of buttonhole and chain stitch, with patches of denim, velvet and handwoven cloth underneath. His motivation is unknown – sewing could have been a way to escape loneliness after his wife's death – but whatever his reason, the ten large cloths he created, with their snippets of text and images of animals and birds, are unique and important records of one ordinary man's life. (Nine of his ten known works reside at the Museum of International Folk Art, Santa Fe.)

In India, the hand-worked applique cloths made by Bihari women from the 1990s onwards act as narrative documents of their lives. They bring to the fore many everyday, overlooked tasks and events, ranging from collecting

Respect and Protect Quilt (2009) | photo Adrian Hunter

and drying cow dung for fuel, to visits from World Health Organisation workers sent to the villages to explain about the spread of AIDS and promote condom awareness.

Respect and Protect (2009)

This project was developed as an Arts and Science partnership project with Joanna Verran, Professor of Microbiology at MMU. We shared an interest in public engagement, having both developed different forms of creative projects as a way of sharing knowledge regarding accessible and inclusive methods when working with the public.

Joanna ran the Bad Bugs Book Club, which met regularly to discuss fiction that explored infectious diseases. The range of books discussed was vast, including *Nemesis* by Philip Roth and Victoria Hislop's *The Island*. Each provoked debate and discussion and, since Covid-19, the book club had grown in size.

The book for December 2009 was Will Self's *Dorian*, a contemporary novel about AIDS. To attract a different audience and offer a tactile response, we developed a plan for a community quilt that would raise awareness of AIDS in the 2000s, drawing

connecting threads

Sample for Respect and Protect (2009)
photo David Bennett

on The NAMES Project, launched in 1985 by the American AIDS and LGBT rights activist, Cleve Jones. When Jones stitched a panel for his friend Marvin Feldman who had died from AIDS many thousands across the world followed suit, stitching coffin-sized quilts in memory of their loved ones.
The intention was to open up conversations and generate better understanding of the current issues affecting people and families living with AIDS and HIV. The first immediate challenge, however, was to ensure that we designed a quilt that was accessible and engaging, so as to allow and encourage as many different communities as possible to be involved.

We received a small grant from the Society for General Microbiology to facilitate some workshops and help with the cost of materials. The deadline was tight – just six weeks to make the resolved quilt in time for World AIDS Day on 1 December. This time frame also included getting groups on board, securing venues and, of course, designing a quilt that could be made by anyone in a group workshop setting.

Research and sampling began in early October. After some searching online, we decided on a design inspired by a recent HIV and AIDS campaign. What resonated most was the term 'Respect and Protect', a broadly inclusive and simple phrase that also felt pertinent and important beyond its direct link with AIDS.

With these words as a starting point, designing and testing began. Using a one-metre square cloth, I cut out letters

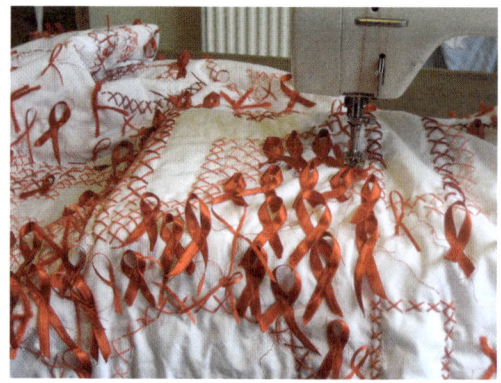

Machining red crosses onto the quilt (2009)
photo Adrian Hunter

in different sizes and laid them on the fabric to explore compositions. A white cross referencing the motif found on first aid kits and traditional grave markers, was placed at the centre of the quilt alongside the key words 'Respect and Protect'. I also spent some time experimenting with red thread and cross stitches, both of which connected the fund-raising World AIDS Day motif (a red ribbon) to our quilt. Cross stitches are an identifying feature of traditional embroidered samplers. Originally produced by skilled needleworkers as a method of recording decorative stitches and patterns, samplers also developed as a learning exercise for girls denied formal education because of their sex in centuries past. Throughout history, the use of a cross as an identifier was also significant within society and is still used today, not least when we mark our ballot papers at the polls.

We also included some larger crosses made from red ribbon. These crosses provided another link back to the AIDS fundraiser but, more importantly, offered an additional way of filling the quilt's surface just in case there were not enough stitched crosses. This was a belt and braces approach – experience has shown that having alternative options in place reduces stress during uncertain undertakings such as this. Attaching larger ribbons using a sewing machine also helped fill-in the central area of the quilt, a space that is hard to reach and work on in a group activity.

Lynn Setterington and Jo Verran, World AIDS Day (2009) | photo Adrian Hunter

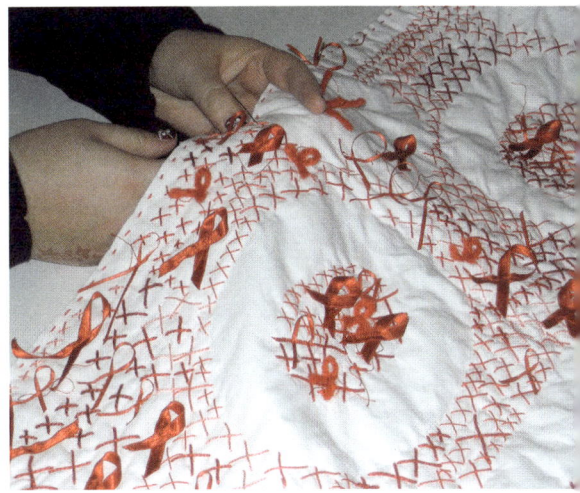

Detail, Respect and Protect workshop (2009)
photo Adrian Hunter

connecting threads

Workshop with art and science students at MMU on World AIDS Day | photo Lauren Steeper

Workshop with art and science students at MMU on World AIDS Day | photo Lauren Steeper

With time restraints a constant in this project, I turned to groups and partners I already knew and who I was confident would be experienced working on this kind of community-led project. (In my experience, it takes time and patience to build trust and understanding and bring new groups on board.) This included the Whitworth Art Gallery which had workshop space, a large audience and was familiar with my past work. Manchester MIND, Cedar Mount Academy and Special Collections at MMU were also invited to be involved in the stitch workshops. Art and science students at MMU were invited to work on the quilt on World AIDS Day itself as a way of bringing students together from different disciplines, and sharing the initiative across the university campus. Each stage of making was documented as a way to recall the different workshops and venues, but also as a prompt to remember how the quilt took shape during the different community-focused phases.

As with Stitching Up Oxford Road, the workshop sessions provided an opportunity to share different types of information and knowledge, with printed information about the AIDS virus and the NAMES Project on hand for those who wanted to know more. Once the quilt was complete, Joanne Verran shared it in several microbiology events and it was displayed alongside photographs of the workshops in an exhibition at the People's History Museum, Manchester for World AIDS Day, December 2011.

Safety Net with Nick Tunnicliffe, Chapel Street, Salford (2021) | photo Mary Stark

In 2012 the quilt was donated to the HIV and sexual health charity, the Terrence Higgins Trust, Islington, London where it is on permanent public display.

Safety Net (2021)

Using the World Health Organisation's slogan, 'There is no health without mental health', these artworks made from repurposed debris net were designed, created and installed across two major thoroughfares in Manchester and Salford in October 2021 to mark World Mental Health Day.

The workload was shared with two partner organisations, the Manchester based construction companies Tunny Scaffolding and the Northhold Group, along with others concerned with improving our wellbeing including the young people's mental health charity, 42nd Street and a number of Textile in Practice (TiP) students from MMU. As well as helping with design ideas, these partnerships proved to be a positive way to share knowledge and skills and raise awareness of the challenges of poor mental health. The artwork as in the public domain but it was directed chiefly towards the construction industry which, according to figures from the Office of National Statistics, has a suicide rate of more than three times the national average. That is the highest of any profession in the UK.

An initial test piece on how to use the debris net in an outdoor installation began in March 2020 as lockdown took hold. This was a partnership with Conlon Construction on a building site at MMU to see if the idea was feasible and practical in the real world. (A digital rendition of the text-based work was created so see how the letters would be distributed on the building sites).

connecting threads

Safety Net on Oldham Road, Manchester (2021)
photo Lynn Setterington

connecting threads

Safety Net banners at Museum Dr Guislain, Gent, Belguim (2022) | photo Lynn Setterington

Testing the banners in courtyard at MMU (2021)
photo Lynn Setterington

Following the success of the first trial, and as lockdown eased, the search began for a new higher profile location and a new construction partner, as Conlon did not have a site suitable in Manchester. After a few enquires a local company agreed to help with the project both to find a site and also install the artwork. They had good credentials in sustainability and health and wellbeing and so all seemed to be progressing well. They requested we use flame-retardant net as this was required for their health and safety building regulations, so a second iteration of the text 'There is no Health' was made with help of TiP graduates, Elle Samson and Harinder Kooner.

Everything seemed to be going to plan until, just days before the installation date, when we consulted about the installation of the work with the building's owner, who said we would not be able to use the site after all. Further discussions ensued and investigations revealed that the building was covered in cladding and, understandably, the owner felt the scaffolding drew unwanted attention to the location.

We had no choice but to step back and rethink the project. The original plan had been to install the work in July, leaving the lettering in place over the summer. With no site for the artwork, that clearly was not going to be possible so we came up with the idea of launching on World Mental Health Day itself; 10 October.

However, there was a positive in the change of events and the new date resonated with the work's theme; and the break was useful, allowing us to return with fresh eyes and a different perspective. We realised that there had been a major miscommunication and, for whatever reason, the construction company did not understand the scale or significance of the work. Rather than trying to build bridges, we decided to search for a suitable building first and then find the company working on it. This strategy gave us far more control over the selection process.

Our travels around Manchester were productive and we discovered several new possible venues. One was a classic old red brick building covered in green debris net on Salford's Chapel Street. It was on a busy road into the city in an area developing fast, with new builds sitting alongside older properties. The site seemed to be out of use, but there was a discreet sign on the scaffolding structure with a Manchester phone number and the name 'Tunny'.

Another interesting location was on Oldham Road in Ancoats, central Manchester. Like the Chapel Street site, it was on a busy route into the city, but this was a new build covered in bold, red and blue-striped debris netting. It was also an active site, busy with construction workers. Because of the setback with the earlier site, we decided to approach both companies to gauge interest in our project and keep our options open. Within

Testing the banners on a building site (2020)
photo Lynn Setterington

a few days they had both responded positively. In a telephone conversation, Tunny also mentioned the importance of this work, explaining they had lost a scaffolder to suicide in the last year. As we had already created two sets of banners spelling out the key slogan, we decided to work with both companies on both sites. Most of the making work was already done, so all we needed to do was hand over the text to the construction companies to install. We had learned from our experience with the previous location and so contacted the owners of the buildings ourselves to check they were happy to work with us. The Tunny site was owned by Salford Cathedral which said yes, provided Tunny installed the banners. The Northhold Group were also keen to proceed with the installation on their Oldham Road site.

We decided to use the flame-retardant net lettering for the Salford site. This was because the aesthetic there was quite calm

Ellie Samson laying out the net banners (2021)
photo Lynn Setterington

Oldham Road banners showing the different colourways (2021) | photo Lynn Setterington

and the four colours and wording would stand out well against the green net already in place. In contrast, for the Oldham Road site, with its red and blue-striped net, we used the mixed letters created for the test site with Conlon. More ad hoc in shape and style and involving a wide range of colours and fonts, we felt they would sit well against the busy site.

We agreed to hand the letters over to the construction companies for installation in early October. Both scaffolding teams were given copies of the photoshop visualisations we had made showing the positioning of each letter. Tunny had expressed a personal interest in the story of suicide and had put aside a specific day for their scaffolders to install the work when the site was not in use, so we decided to film the process at Chapel Street. The Northhold site was an active working space which meant the team had to work very differently and install its lettering over a three day period, as and when scaffolders were available.

The banners on Chapel Street, Salford and Oldham Road, Manchester were seen by around 100,000 passers-by and the three-minute film provides a legacy of the work, enabling the project to be shared with different audiences, both nationally and internationally. Staging such an arresting visual intervention in the heart of the city highlighted this important issue to the construction industry and helped to bring

connecting threads

it to the attention of the wider public. The two sites had very different feels, characters and purposes, but these two interventions highlight how collaborative working can bring together mental health and creativity to good effect and use overlooked spaces in the urban environment.

The final word should go to Tunny Scaffold Director, Lenny Tunnicliffe, who commented: 'In 2021, Lynn asked if Tunny would display the creative work she had produced to raise awareness of poor mental health in the construction industry. This was an easy yes. The banner stated: There is no health without mental health, which we put up as it is such an important message for us in the construction industry. Back in 2021, there were 507 suicides in the construction industry alone. Prior to this point, we had lost two of our own scaffolders to suicide, and have sadly lost another young scaffolder earlier this year. Lynn's work is extremely valuable and the importance of raising these issues is absolutely vital as there is so little talked about it, without being prompted. I do hope Lynn can be supported and can continue to raise awareness.'

Tunny scaffolders installing on Chapel Street (2021)
photo Mary Stark

Lynn Setterington and Tunny scaffolders (2021)
photo Mary Stark

connecting threads

Living with Loss (2020)

Living with Loss is a modern-day sampler, a text-based cloth made from repurposed materials from the construction industry. The black and white debris net was cut into strips and used as the thread to stitch with, while the pink rendering mesh (donated by a construction worker on a building site in Manchester) provides a vibrant ground.

The unusual materials work together in this piece to create something new that also, references its origins: a hand-worked sampler. Made in 2020 in the midst of the Covid-19 crisis, it is both a physical representation of those dark days and also a reminder of how, collectively, we dealt with sorrow. The embroidered text is a simple, direct statement about loss and bereavement, questioning how we navigate such universal and complex issues.

The British are known for their reserved nature, especially on the subject of grief and death. This textile confronts the viewer directly drawing attention to the reality that this is an issue that affects us all. Leaving the stitching incomplete also serves as a reminder that things in life are often left unresolved and highlights the challenge in knowing when to stop.

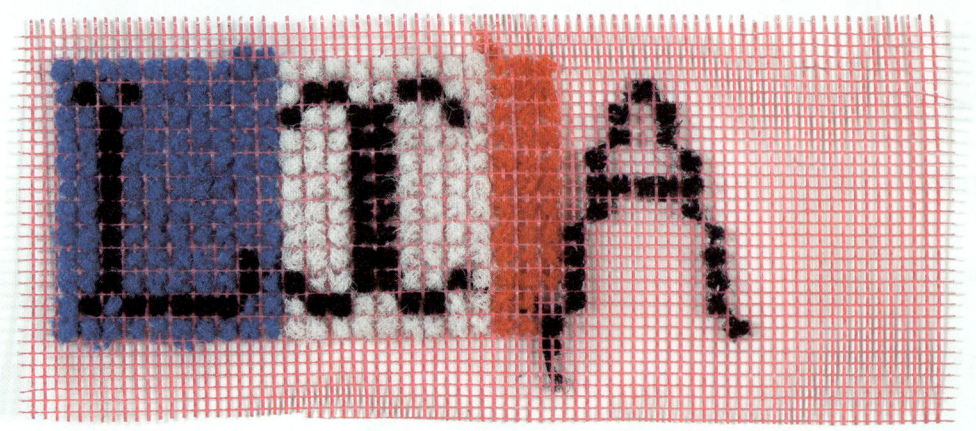

Testing colourways using debris net | photo Lynn Setterington

Living With Loss, hand-stitched sampler using debris net (2020) | photo Lynn Setterington

Running a community project

This is not a 'how to' book, but when working with a community or group, some simple guidelines can help circumvent issues later. It is a good idea to define your outcomes before you begin – have a clear narrative and idea and lay out the aims and objectives from the start so everyone is on board good. Try to establish parameters for the project as much as possible, the timescale, numbers involved and where the resulting work will be shown and highlight what will partner organisations and participants will gain from being involved. Then define your methodologies – how will you make the artwork, what is its theme and what are the making strategies? Try to estimate the costs involved. Factors include the location of the workshops and accessibility, the make-up of the groups, whether can you leave materials and equipment on site. How many people will be in the sessions and is your idea feasible and practical? Accessibility, flexibility and adaptability are key to the success of any project.

left: **Coloured debris net for hand stitch workshop (2021)**
photo Lynn Setterington

Resources

- Get a sense of the community partners involved at the beginning so that ideas marry together for a successful outcome. Talk to stakeholders to understand the people who might want to be involved. Do a pilot workshop if possible or observe one so you see how the group operates. Find out if those involved have done creative projects before and if so what.

- Try and make time to test and sample ideas independently before a project starts. It will pay off in the end.

- Check venues before the work begins to ensure that the room and tables are arranged in an open and accessible layout, and are suitable for working. (This is a helpful first step so that materials, equipment, skills and ideas can be shared.) People need to feel comfortable and be able move around the space easily.

- Good light and access to a kettle to make hot drinks are also helpful.

- A basic introduction to threading a needle is an easy win in a shared setting where people may not have sewn before.

- Visual textile-related publications or journals are also a useful addition to the session so people can read related information at their leisure and learn more about your work and past projects.

- Likewise, having relevant stitch samples and textile processes is a good way to share knowledge. If these are available throughout the session, people can look at them at any stage during the workshop. Including variations in yarns, colours and scales demonstrates how the work can and may evolve and is a positive way to engage new audiences.

Recording and documenting

- How will you make a record of participatory sessions? The many unseen values in shared making should (ideally) be recorded in some way so that these hidden benefits can be acknowledged alongside the resulting textile. Successful methods we have used include photography, film and face-to-face interviews. You can collect sound bites from people or create a focus group to share comments after the workshops.

- Think about sharing outcomes in journal or magazine articles, or other venues to show the resulting work, can be online in a blog, on Instagram or perhaps in a touring exhibition.

- Share the photos with the group and individuals so they are included in the project and be prepared to delete images if they do not like any. Always make sure participants are happy to be recorded before you do it, as not everyone is.

Large-scale stitch sample (2021)
photo Lynn Setterington

Glossary of terms

Kantha
Kantha embroidery and quilting originates in the Bengal area in what is now Bangladesh and India. Early traditional kanthas made in the late 19th and early 20th centuries were created from old saris and dhotis pieced together to make a new top cloth, the size and shape depends on their intended use. They are made exclusively by women and constitute an important part of traditional Bengali folk art.

Quilt
A quilt is usually composed of three basic elements: a top layer, which is usually pieced or has a sewn surface decoration; an inner layer of padding; and a back layer. The quilting is a type of stitching – by hand or machine – that goes through the layers to join the materials and make a more robust textile.

Patchwork
A pieced cloth often stitched together from scraps of cloth. It can be quilted by adding layers of fabric under the top cloth.

Signature Cloth
A textile where the predominant surface decoration is composed of signatures, sewn either by hand or machine. A signature cloth is one fabric with signatures sewn on to the surface. A signature quilt is made up of layers of fabrics, the quilting process adds a textured quality and is created either by hand stitch or by machine or digital stitch.

Suffolk puff
This is a traditional textile process, which has a long history, possibly dating back to the 17th century. It can also be referred to as a Devon puff, these British names reflect its origins and the use of fleece or wool to stuff the circles of cloth to make them more robust and provide warmth. In the US they are known as a yo-yos.

Debris net
This is the ubiquitous material used on building sites across the UK (and the world) to prevent debris falling onto traffic and passersby. It comes in a wide range of colours and is a knitted fibre made from plastic.

Khadi cloth
This is a type of hand-woven natural fabric produced in India. It is generally a coarse cloth and originated in the early 20th century. The name was coined by Mahatma Gandi to support self-sufficiency and the freedom struggle in the Indian sub-continent.

Faggoting machine
This is a specialist sewing machine that creates a type of decorative insertion stitch to connect fabrics. It creates a lace like pattern or stitch working between the edges of cloth and was especially popular on lingerie, collars and sleeves. It was developed for use in the fashion industry and the workshops at MMU still have a wide range of unusual specialist sewing machines which are used in new and inventive ways by current students.

Work in collections

2023   Dominic Cummings, Blue Plaque – MMU Special Collections

2019   Self Portrait – Quilters Guild of the UK

2017   Stitching Up Oxford Road – Whitworth Art Gallery, Manchester

2016   Threads of Identity – Burnage Academy for Boys, Manchester.

2013   Please Sign Here – Touchstones Gallery, Rochdale, Lancashire

2013   Nine Objects – Denver Museum of Art, Colorado, USA

2012   Respect and Protect – Terrence Higgins Trust, London

2008   Tree of Life – Nowgen (Genetic Research Centre), Manchester

2007   Centenary Banner – Alma Park Primary School, Manchester

2006   Women's Community Banner – Gallery Oldham, Banner Collection

2006   Mum's are Heroes, Paradise, New Life and A Night In –
University of Nebraska, International Quilt Museum

2004   Family Trees – Stoneyholme and St Stephen's Primary Schools, Burnley

2000   Transport Banner – People's History Museum, Manchester

1998   Tools of the Trade – Oldham Museum and Art Gallery, Oldham

1997   The Bathroom Shelf & Whitework Quilt – Victoria and Albert Museum

1997   Kitchen Utensils – Bedfordshire Schools' Art Collection, Bedfordshire

1997   Quilted Map – Science and Industry Museum, Manchester

1996   Unsung Heroes – Shipley Art Gallery, Gateshead

1996   Azadi – Harris Museum, Preston

1995   Wash Day Blues – Embroiderers' Guild of the UK

1994   Sowing Seed – Whitworth Art Gallery, Manchester

1993   DIY – Crafts Council, London

Installing over-sized cross stitches, Ruthin Craft Centre car park

'Lynn Setterington is an extremely important artist working on the edges of politics and ethnography.'

Jane Webb

Head of School for Cross Faculty Studies, Warwick University